Violence in the Media

Other Books in the Current Controversies Series:

Violence in the Media

James D. Torr, *Book Editor*

David Bender, *Publisher*
Bruno Leone, *Executive Editor*

Bonnie Szumski, *Editorial Director*
Stuart B. Miller, *Managing Editor*

CURRENT CONTROVERSIES

Cover photo: Corbis

Library of Congress Cataloging-in-Publication Data

Violence in the media / book editor, James D. Torr.
       p. cm. — (Current controversies)
    Includes bibliographical references and index.
    ISBN 0-7377-0455-1 (pbk. : alk. paper) — ISBN 0-7377-0456-X
(lib. bdg. : alk. paper)
    1. Violence in mass media. I. Torr, James D., 1974–   . II. Series.

P96.V5 V563   2001
303.6'0973—dc21   00-037206
                                                              CIP

©2001 by Greenhaven Press, Inc., PO Box 289009, San Diego, CA 92198-9009
Printed in the U.S.A.

Every effort has been made to trace the owners of copyrighted material.

Contents

Chapter 1: How Serious Is the Problem of Violence in the Media?

Violence in the Media Is a Serious Problem

cially for children. Government leaders must work to oppose media violence—not via censorship, but rather by speaking out against the irresponsible practices of Hollywood and the TV industry, as Bill Clinton has
already done.

The Problem of Media Violence Is Exaggerated

Violence in popular entertainment may be objectionable, but the Supreme
Court has consistently ruled that it is nevertheless protected by the First
Amendment right to free speech. Carving out an exception in the First
Amendment for violent media would subject many valuable works that
contain violent imagery—including the Bible and much of classic literature—to censorship. From a constitutional perspective, infringing on the
right to bear arms would be a much more logical way to reduce violence
than infringing on the First Amendment would be.

Since blaming violence on lack of gun control is politically unpopular in
America, the news media have instead targeted violence in popular entertainment. However, the idea that media violence can make someone commit a crime contradicts common sense as well as research showing that
people in other countries, who enjoy the same movies and TV shows as
Americans, have much lower rates of violence. The step these other countries have taken that America has not is to strictly regulate the availability
of guns.

There is no arguing with the claim that violence in the media is pervasive,
objectionable, and may even inspire some people to commit actual violence. However, a fact that is often overlooked is that Americans in general enjoy violent entertainment—it has not been foisted upon them by
the entertainment industry. Since violent movies and TV shows mirror
the violence that is rampant in their society, it is no surprise that Americans are attracted to them.

Chapter 2: Does Violence in the Media Make Children and Teenagers More Violent?

Yes: Violence in the Media Makes Children Violent

Hollywood and the television industries glamorize guns and murder, and
market this violent imagery specifically to teens. There is no question that
this screen violence has a serious effect on children's propensity to
behave violently later in life. Up until age nineteen, children and teens
exposed to violence in the media are more likely to view violence as a
normal behavior and to become criminals themselves.

arrest, and violent deaths than teenagers do. Rather than demonizing teen-agers—and the music and video games they enjoy—perhaps politicians and the media should consider the possibility that popular culture has had a positive effect on teenagers over the past two decades.

Chapter 3: Should Children's Access to Violent Media Be Restricted?

No: Children's Access to Violent Media Should Not Be Restricted

Chapter 4: How Should the Problem of Media Violence Be Addressed?

films—are either impractical or ineffective. The entertainment industry will only respond to financial pressures; one way to apply such pressure is to file lawsuits against the makers of violent movies and video games.

Lawsuits have been filed against the makers of the films *Natural Born Killers* and *The Basketball Diaries* on the grounds that these films incited several murders. These lawsuits are a grave threat to free speech: If artists can be held liable for every possible effect their work might have on an audience, no art is safe. Moreover, these lawsuits send the harmful message that the responsibility for these crimes lies with movies rather than with the actual murderers.

Media violence is undeniably harmful, but it is nevertheless protected by the First Amendment. Therefore, individuals rather than the government must address the problem of media violence. Violent films and television programs are prevalent because they are profitable; if viewers would stop patronizing this type of entertainment, it would not be so pervasive.

Society must stop viewing popular culture as something that can be molded or changed, and instead recognize that the media environment must be navigated. People must become media literate: They must understand that many media messages are harmful or misleading, and manipulative. They must learn how to resist being taken advantage of by the forces that control television, movies, and other mass media.

Violent stories dominate the mass media not because they are the most popular type of entertainment (nonviolent television programs are consistently the most popular in the U.S. market), but because they are the type of entertainment that can most easily be sold to foreign markets, since the theme of violence crosses cultural barriers. To reverse this pattern, a coalition of citizens and organizations should work to oppose the domination of the media by large conglomerates.

Government has a role to play in helping citizens to mobilize against media violence. Canada and Norway are examples of how governments can initiate broad antiviolence campaigns. To a much greater extent than the United States has, the governments of Canada and Norway have worked to increase media literacy, institute the V-chip, and provide funding for quality children's programming.

Foreword

By definition, controversies are "discussions of questions in which opposing opinions clash" (Webster's Twentieth Century Dictionary Unabridged). Few would deny that controversies are a pervasive part of the human condition and exist on virtually every level of human enterprise. Controversies transpire between individuals and among groups, within nations and between nations. Controversies supply the grist necessary for progress by providing challenges and challengers to the status quo. They also create atmospheres where strife and warfare can flourish. A world without controversies would be a peaceful world; but it also would be, by and large, static and prosaic.

The Series' Purpose

The purpose of the Current Controversies series is to explore many of the social, political, and economic controversies dominating the national and international scenes today. Titles selected for inclusion in the series are highly focused and specific. For example, from the larger category of criminal justice, Current Controversies deals with specific topics such as police brutality, gun control, white collar crime, and others. The debates in Current Controversies also are presented in a useful, timeless fashion. Articles and book excerpts included in each title are selected if they contribute valuable, long-range ideas to the overall debate. And wherever possible, current information is enhanced with historical documents and other relevant materials. Thus, while individual titles are current in focus, every effort is made to ensure that they will not become quickly outdated. Books in the Current Controversies series will remain important resources for librarians, teachers, and students for many years.

In addition to keeping the titles focused and specific, great care is taken in the editorial format of each book in the series. Book introductions and chapter prefaces are offered to provide background material for readers. Chapters are organized around several key questions that are answered with diverse opinions representing all points on the political spectrum. Materials in each chapter include opinions in which authors clearly disagree as well as alternative opinions in which authors may agree on a broader issue but disagree on the possible solutions. In this way, the content of each volume in Current Controversies mirrors the mosaic of opinions encountered in society. Readers will quickly realize that there are many viable answers to these complex issues. By questioning each author's conclusions, students and casual readers can begin to develop the critical thinking skills so important to evaluating opinionated material.

Current Controversies is also ideal for controlled research. Each anthology in the series is composed of primary sources taken from a wide gamut of informational categories including periodicals, newspapers, books, United States and foreign government documents, and the publications of private and public organizations. Readers will find factual support for reports, debates, and research papers covering all areas of important issues. In addition, an annotated table of contents, an index, a book and periodical bibliography, and a list of organizations to contact are included in each book to expedite further research.

Perhaps more than ever before in history, people are confronted with diverse and contradictory information. During the Persian Gulf War, for example, the public was not only treated to minute-to-minute coverage of the war, it was also inundated with critiques of the coverage and countless analyses of the factors motivating U.S. involvement. Being able to sort through the plethora of opinions accompanying today's major issues, and to draw one's own conclusions, can be a complicated and frustrating struggle. It is the editors' hope that Current Controversies will help readers with this struggle.

Greenhaven Press anthologies primarily consist of previously published material taken from a variety of sources, including periodicals, books, scholarly journals, newspapers, government documents, and position papers from private and public organizations. These original sources are often edited for length and to ensure their accessibility for a young adult audience. The anthology editors also change the original titles of these works in order to clearly present the main thesis of each viewpoint and to explicitly indicate the opinion presented in the viewpoint. These alterations are made in consideration of both the reading and comprehension levels of a young adult audience. Every effort is made to ensure that Greenhaven Press accurately reflects the original intent of the authors included in this anthology.

"'Never was a culture so filled with full-color images of violence as ours is now.'"

Introduction

People have always been drawn to spectacles of violence. As Sissela Bok points out in her book *Mayhem: Violence as Public Entertainment*, the ancient Romans forced slaves and convicts to fight wild animals to the death before roaring crowds as a matter of public policy. "Violent spectacles kept the citizenry distracted, engaged, and entertained and . . . provided the continuing acculturation to violence needed by a warrior state."

In comparison to the ancient Romans, modern Americans seem far less bloodthirsty. After all, writes Ray Surette, author of *The Media and Criminal Justice Policy*, "We do not kill real people in public spectacles." Nevertheless, warns Surette, the level of *fictional* violence in American culture is staggering: "We have eased the access to fantasy slaughter far beyond anything the Romans dreamed of."

According to researcher George Gerbner, "Never was a culture so filled with full-color images of violence as ours is now." Gerbner's Cultural Indicators project, which has monitored TV violence since 1968, estimates that the average American child views more than 8,000 murders and 100,000 acts of violence on television during the elementary school years. A 1992 study in the *Journal of the American Medical Association* found that the typical American child will witness 40,000 on-screen murders by the age of eighteen.

Concern about violence in the media predates television—in the nineteenth century social critics warned that juveniles were mimicking the violence they read about in newspapers, and in the 1920s there was considerable outrage over what was considered "rampant" violence and lawlessness in the movies. However, the most extensive research on media violence has focused on television violence, beginning in 1968 when President Lyndon Johnson convened the National Commission on the Causes and Prevention of Violence and commissioned Gerbner to analyze the content of television shows. Gerbner's research was influential in the landmark 1972 Surgeon General's report on media violence, which found evidence of "a causal relation between viewing violence on television and aggressive behavior."

Public outcries against media violence are closely tied to rising levels of violent crime. For example, levels of violent juvenile crime peaked in 1995. Calls for government action to curb TV violence followed a similar trend, and in 1996 Congress passed the Telecommunications Act, which, among its provisions, required the TV broadcasting industry to develop a voluntary ratings system. The act also required that by the year 2000 all televisions manufactured in the United States would include the V-chip, an electronic device that would allow parents to block out programs with violent content.

But just as the furor over media violence seemed to be fading, however, another trend in youth violence captured society's attention: a wave of school shootings, in which middle and high school students killed their classmates and teachers. On October 1, 1997, sixteen-year-old Luke Woodham killed two students in his Pearl, Mississippi, high school. On December 1 of that year fourteen-year-old Michael Carneal killed three students and wounded eight others in West Paducah, Kentucky. On March 24, 1998, thirteen-year-old Mitchell Johnson and eleven-year-old Andrew Golden killed four students and one teacher, and wounded fifteen others, in Jonesboro, Arkansas. And on May 21, 1998, fifteen-year-old Kip Kinkel opened fire in his high school in Springfield, Oregon, after murdering both his parents the previous night.

After all these tragedies, the nation was further horrified by the massacre at Columbine High School in Littleton, Colorado: On April 20, 1999, eighteen-year-old Eric Harris and seventeen-year-old Dylan Klebold, armed with semi-automatic weapons and explosives, killed thirteen people before committing suicide. Evidence that the two students had extensively planned their shooting spree, and in fact intended to kill far more than fifteen people, left the country searching for an explanation of what could have driven Harris and Klebold, as well as the other perpetrators of school shootings, to such violence.

Attention soon turned to the types of entertainment these students had immersed themselves in. Some cited the music Harris and Klebold listened to, which included shock rocker Marilyn Manson. Others noted that many of the school shooters played violent "first-person shooter" video games such as Doom, in which the player's goal is to literally shoot anything that moves. Others argued that movies and TV in general glamorize violence, citing, for example, 1995's *The Basketball Diaries*, in which Leonardo DiCaprio's character graphically fantasizes about going on a shooting spree in his high school.

But beyond these specific examples of violent imagery, critics of media violence once again returned to the 1972 Surgeon General's report and all the other research that has been done on the link between fictional and real-life violence. As Arnold P. Goldstein explains in his book, *Violence in America*, many of these studies have found a link between the viewing of violence and three long-term effects:

1. The copycat effect. A minority of viewers will mimic the violence they see on the screen. For example, the 1995 movie *Money Train* portrayed a killer who set fire to subway booths, killing the attendants inside. In New York in December of that year, two youths copied the crime.
2. The desensitization effect. Audiences eventually adapt to a certain level of on-screen violence, and ever-more graphic depictions of violence are nec-

essary to shock them. A classic example is action or horror movie sequels, which almost always feature more gore and a higher "body count" than their predecessors.

3. The "victim effect" (which George Gerbner has also described as "Mean World Syndrome"). Elizabeth Thomlan, of the Center for Media Literacy, explains that constant exposure to violence in the media may lead people "to believe that violence is everywhere and that they must be afraid." Many critics feel that this is the most insidious effect of violence in the media, since it conceivably affects everyone, not just those individuals who go on to commit violence. "Heavy viewers [of TV violence]," writes the *Atlantic Monthly*'s Scott Stossel, "tend to favor more law-and-order measures: capital punishment, . . . the building of new prisons, and so forth."

However, while most social scientists accept the *correlation* between media violence and actual violence, many dispute the idea that exposure to fictional violence *causes* people to become violent. In this view, those who "copycat" crimes they have seen in movies are prone to violence to begin with. And it may be that instead of people being made violent by entertainment, violent individuals may simply prefer violent entertainment. "There is no convincing, in fact, no substantial evidence that television violence affects aggression or crime," writes psychology professor Jonathan Freedman.

Many commentators have specifically rejected the notion that Eric Harris's and Dylan Klebold's exposure to violence in the media caused them to become killers. "The reason the Colorado shootings became news around the world," writes Joe Saltzman of *USA Today*, "was the rarity, the unusual how-could-this-have-happened nature of the story. . . . Logic dictates that, if movies, television, video games, and the Internet are responsible for this kind of behavior, then why is it so unusual?"

But critics of media violence respond that although violent video games or movies were obviously not the only antisocial forces at work in the killers' lives, the violent entertainment they were so obsessed with certainly could not have been healthy. In this view, violent entertainment is only one part—along with guns and the American tendency to value competition and individuality over cooperation and community—of a "culture of violence" that afflicts America.

One symptom of America's "culture of violence" is that the United States has the highest levels of homicide of all the industrialized nations in the world. The authors in *Violence in the Media: Current Controversies* debate what role violence in entertainment plays in contributing to the level of violence in society in the following chapters: How Serious Is the Problem of Violence in the Media? Does Violence in the Media Make Children and Teenagers More Violent? Should Children's Access to Violent Media Be Restricted? How Should the Problem of Media Violence Be Addressed?

Chapter 1

How Serious Is the Problem of Violence in the Media?

Chapter Preface

"For at least two decades, experts have warned that television, movies, music, and other entertainment media are desensitizing young people to violence and death," writes Judith A. Reisman, president of the Institute for Media Education. "Murder, rape, and physical assault are common fare in movies and award-winning television drama, and some popular music genres have taken to glorifying sex, violence, murder, and even suicide," she warns, echoing a common view that the level of violence in popular culture has reached crisis proportions. "Most parents," writes former Secretary of Education William Bennett, "although they are not . . . revolting in the streets, are deeply worried. They feel as if they are swimming upstream, fighting against faceless television, movie, and music executives who are fighting against them. This is a very serious problem."

But many writers and artists argue that parents and lawmakers must resist the temptation to label all media violence as harmful or worthless. They point out that violence can be an important ingredient in dramatic storytelling. Writer David Link notes that "Anyone with any historical perspective knows that violence appears to be an eternal theme, from Homer and the Bible right up to Schwarzenegger and Sylvester Stallone." Link explains, "Violence and danger are among the tools I have as a fiction maker, alongside sex, religion, truth, authority, honor, and every other human characteristic—strengths and weaknesses alike." Moreover, Link believes that television programs that feature violence often send a positive moral message: "On television in particular, the overwhelming majority of violent acts are committed by someone clearly identifiable as the antagonist. In cases where a protagonist engages in violence, that violence is either legitimized by justice or righteousness, or it is a necessary response to a violent provocation."

The distinction between responsible and irresponsible portrayals of violence is a prominent theme in the debate over media violence. For example, in a plea to television and movie executives, Bennett asks that they consider the following questions: "Can you understand the difference between gratuitous violence that simply titillates and violence that serves a purpose in telling a larger story? Can you distinguish between *Casino* and *MacBeth*, between *The Basketball Diaries* and *Braveheart*?"

Whether violent entertainment has artistic merit is just one of the issues comprising the controversy over media violence. The authors in the following chapter debate whether the problem of media violence is in fact as bad as critics such as Reisman often claim.

Popular Culture Glorifies Violence

by Kevin Merida and Richard Leiby

About the authors: *Kevin Merida and Richard Leiby are staff writers for the* Washington Post.

In what used to be the dark corners of our culture, there is a prime-time cartoon with a neo-Nazi character, comics that traffic in bestiality, movies that leave teenagers gutted like game, fashion designers who peddle black leather masks and doomsday visions.

It's all in the open now, mass-produced, widely available. Even celebrated. On countless PCs, killing is a sport. And there's Marilyn Manson, a popular singer who named himself after a mass murderer and proclaims he is the Antichrist.

Film, television, music, dress, technology, games: They've become one giant playground filled with accessible evil, darker than ever before.

After any tragedy involving children, the commentators strive to decode the killers, hoping to find cultural signifiers that will somehow explain the carnage. Fifteen dead in a prosperous suburban high school? A clique dubbed the Trenchcoat Mafia connected? The reach for explanation is irresistible.

Some will consult the lyrics of Manson or the German industrial band KMFDM, or cue up the video "The Basketball Diaries." Others will peruse the new comic book "The Trenchcoat Brigade." And did anyone notice that the friend of the killers, being led away Tuesday, April 20, [1999] was wearing a black "South Park" T-shirt featuring the cartoon character Kenny, who is bloodily dispatched in every episode?

And yet any such search for clues may overlook the bigger picture: For young people, the culture at large is bathed in blood and violence—a Grand Guignol, where the more extreme the message, the more over-the-top gruesomeness, the better.

Consider: Of the 11 major movies released on video [between April 6 and April 22, 1999], seven of them have violent themes. Among them: "Apt Pupil," about a high school kid obsessed with Nazism; "American History X," about the rise and fall of a skinhead; and "I Still Know What You Did Last Summer," a teen slasher sequel.

"There's no question in my mind that film and society interrelate," says Douglas Brode, a professor of film at Syracuse University and author of 18 books on the movies. "And not just film, but music, video games, all of it. There is a connection. It may be tangential, it may be tight. Nobody knows for sure."

And so caution and perspective are urged. There are movies about angels and the afterlife, too.

It is surely one of the great debates of this decade: Does the culture simply reflect the dark, decadent times in which we live? Or is society this way because the cultural proprietors have run amok?

Take "Basketball Diaries," the 1995 movie based on writer-rocker Jim Carroll's autobiographical book about his tumble from New York City high school basketball star to heroin addict. In the film there is a dream sequence in which star Leonardo DiCaprio, wearing an ankle-length black leather coat and brandishing a three-foot rifle, walks into his high school classroom and starts blowing away students. One by one. In slow motion. Rock music in the background. Kills his teacher, too. Meanwhile, his friends in the class are high-fiving and laughing.

So is screenwriter Bryan Goluboss an artist drafting from reality, making his screenplay authentic? Or is his creation being copied by real schoolkids in Littleton, Colorado, wearing real trench coats, blowing away their real peers? "Basketball Diaries" already has been cited as a factor in the shooting of three students in West Paducah, Kentucky, two years ago. Authorities said the 14-year-old trigger boy may have planned his attack after watching the movie.

In the wake of this latest tragedy, Brode urges taking a wide look.

"The way I see it," explains Brode, "is there is not more darkness or more lightness than before. It's that everything is more extreme today. The middle is gone. The darkness is darker than before."

In the past six years, as computing power has increased, computer games have become horrifically realistic—and vicious. An entire genre of games, called "first-person shooters," encourages the player to dismember monsters and slay people. The trend began with "Wolfenstein 3D," a game in which an American GI stuck in a Nazi prison must kill Hitler types to

"Film, television, music, dress, technology, games: They've become one giant playground filled with accessible evil, darker than ever before."

survive. Today there are games like "Postal," in which the goal is to slaughter innocent bystanders, including cheerleaders who moan for mercy.

The cover of the game Blood II promises: "Over 30 screamingly fast totally immersive blood-soaked levels! Run a savage gauntlet of multiplayer mayhem from BloodFeud to BloodBath for Maximum BloodShed!"

"They're incredibly violent, and they're the most popular games on PCs right now," says Mike Davila, editorial director of GameWeek, a trade magazine. "The object is to kill people—you see chunks of the body flying in different directions."

Eric Harris, one of the shooters in Colorado, reportedly was an expert player of Doom, a 3-D shooter game introduced in 1994 by id Software of Texas. Doom's marketing strategy was hard to resist: The game was given away over the Internet. Players could customize their killing rooms, selecting from a cache of multiple weapons. They could add new levels by paying for software. At least a half-million copies of Doom were sold or distributed. Doom led to Quake, a $50 game that has sold about 700,000 copies.

The similarity between such high-tech pursuits and the high school slaughter was obvious to Joe Rosenthal, an editor of *Rolling Stone*'s online service: "It's as if these kids were playing a game of Doom, going from room to room, shooting people up, using multiple weapons."

Rosenthal was among those sifting for clues in the lyrics left behind by Harris in his America Online user profile. The lyrics were from an anti-racist German band called KMFDM, which released its final album on Tuesday. Some of the lyrics are brutal, Teutonic and nihilistic—"Iron will . . . Born to kill . . . Son of a gun . . . Master of fate bows to no kingdom or state"—but no more shocking than, say, hard-core rap music or any other forms that have flourished since the advent of punk music in the 1970s.

> *"Everything is more extreme today. The middle is gone. The darkness is darker than before."*

Increasingly, musicians must push the edges of taste, because it's truly difficult to shock their audiences. When your parents grew up with rock-and-roll and still flock to concerts by the Rolling Stones, how do you rebel against them? Some white suburbanites turn to gangsta rap; others immerse themselves in such theatrical genres as "death metal" or "grindcore," which focus on mayhem, mutilation and death. They boast such names as Cannibal Corpse and Visceral Evisceration.

This slide to the shocking takes many forms. You can see it in pro wrestling, whose televised stompfests bring a ratings bonanza. You can see it in cartoons like "South Park" and "Futurama," in which [a recent] episode featured a planet run by robots whose goal is to kill all humans. And in "Family Guy," a cartoon featuring an infant neo-Nazi character who keeps bumping people off.

You can see it in a performance by the artist formerly known as Prince, who on a recent tour performed with a microphone shaped like a handgun. When he sings, it looks as if he's pointing the gun into his mouth, flirting with suicide.

Much of yesterday's armchair analysis dealt with the subculture of Goth music, a genre characterized by gloomy lyrics and a poetic fascination with misery. Goth-rock captures teen angst; it does not promote violence, its adherents say. "If wearing black makes you Goth, then Johnny Cash must be awfully

Goth," notes Sam Rosenthal, owner of the Projekt label, whose "ethereal" Goth acts include Love Spirals Downwards and Black Tape for a Blue Girl.

"There's some confusion in mass media about what Goth is," said his girl-friend, Lisa Feuer, who plays flute in Black Tape for a Blue Girl. "Marilyn Manson is not Goth—I repeat, NOT Goth. NOT GOTH!"

But Manson's fans tend toward that morbidly pale look and an almost Victorian enchantment with gloom. Some, like Feuer, tended not to be popular in high school.

> *"An entire genre of games, called 'first-person shooters,' encourages the player to dismember monsters and slay people."*

"That made me sad, so I found bands like Bauhaus and the Cure, and it was like, misery loves consolation. Those bands were singing about that and it made me feel better about myself." She hastens to add: "I didn't go out and shoot people."

Dark themes pervade the comic book industry too. The trend started in 1986, according to some industry experts, with "Batman: The Dark Night Returns" and "Watchman." In one, Batman ruthlessly kills off bad guys to clean up the city. The other is a murder mystery in which someone keeps snuffing out super-heroes who are discovered to be flawed characters.

"Both were hugely influential," says Joel Pollack, owner of Big Planet Comics in Bethesda. "They both had a very dark vision."

More recently there have been over-the-edge comic books such as "Preacher," in which child abuse and bestiality have been subtexts and obscenities flow with the blood.

Fashion is not exempt, either.

In March of '96, the British designer Alexander McQueen showed his work in New York for the first time. For the setting, he selected a dark synagogue, an imposing structure with sharp angles and filled with white, flickering candles. Amidst a display of corseted jackets and asymmetrical hemlines were acces-sories such as a half-mask adorned with a crucifix and a silver "crown of thorns." Subsequent collections have included metal leg braces and arm cuffs.

In April of '97, American designer Anna Sui held her show in an empty church on Central Park West. She draped the altar area with crimson cloth and lit hundreds of red votives. The collection included a model wearing tiny blood-red beaded Devil horns.

This year, designers from Helmut Lang to Maurice Malone showed gar-ments—a black, leather face mask, for instance—that could be described as pessimistic urban armor.

The fashion industry has for years been enamored with the dark side of life, the murky underground and a nihilistic sensibility. Indeed, as more established designers several years ago began to shed the constraints of minimalism and to adopt a more lively, highly decorated style, a generation of young designers has stepped into the foreground bringing a doomsday vision of the future. Their work is marked by a black palette, a fetishistic relationship to sexuality and a view of the environment as hostile, even deadly.

This dark view of the world is one of the most powerful examples of the way in which fashion acts as a sponge, with designers pointedly absorbing inspiration from music, the nightclubs, the street. A designer such as Sui has always had one ear turned toward the radio as a way to fuel her creativity. And designers such as Olivier Theyskens, Veronique Branquinho and McQueen have all grown up on a steady diet of televised gunplay, car crashes and eroticized violence. That has been the nature of popular culture for more than a decade. And as the writer Richard Buckley noted earlier this year, it is only natural that this generation's version of fashion should be not only shocking and aggressive, but also fatalistic.

Just like the rest of the culture.

Violence on Television Is a Serious Problem

by James T. Hamilton

About the author: *James T. Hamilton is a professor of public policy, economics, and political science at Duke University and the author of* Channeling Violence: The Economic Market for Violent Television Programming.

Editor's note: The following viewpoint is excerpted from Hamilton's May 1999 testimony before the Senate Committee on Commerce, Science, and Transportation, at a hearing on TV violence.

Television violence is at its core a problem of pollution. Programmers and advertisers use violent content to target television's most valuable demographic, viewers age 18–34. The executives who schedule violence to garner ratings and profits do not take into account the full impact on society of their actions. Research shows that television violence does increase levels of aggression, fear, and desensitization among some who consume it. The strongest impacts are on the youngest viewers. Children are not the target of advertisers on most violent programs. But their exposure to violent images can lead to social damages not factored into decisions about when to air programs and where to draw the line on content.

Common Defenses of TV Violence

In writing a book on the market for violent programming, I (understandably) found few people in the entertainment industry willing to agree their products generate cultural pollution. Media officials often deflect criticisms of their programs with a standard set of responses, which I came to view as the "Top 5 Reasons Why TV Violence Is Not a Problem."

1. *We use violence on television to tell, not sell, stories.* Television executives link the use of violence to narrative needs. In hearings before Congress, network executives have denied that they use violence to earn ratings. Yet I found in my research on programming strategies that every channel type uses violence to gain viewers:

Excerpted from testimony given by James T. Hamilton before the Senate Committee on Commerce, Science, and Transportation, May 18, 1999.

- During the sweeps periods, the four major broadcast networks were much more likely to air movies that deal with murder, focus on tales of family crime, and feature family crime or murder stories based on real-life incidents. Nearly a third of network movies during sweeps periods dealt with murder. The Fox network, which often aired movies starting at 8 P.M., increased its use of violent movies from 42% to 84% during sweeps.
- When ABC aired *Monday Night Football,* the basic cable channel TBS dropped its use of violent movies on Monday nights. The percentage of violent movies declined on this channel from 92% to 65% of the films shown. When football season ended and male viewers were up for grabs, the violent movies returned.
- When *Seinfeld* dominated ratings on Thursday evenings, HBO had a strategy known internally as 'Testosterone Thursday,' in which it programmed low-quality violent films at 9 P.M. to attract male viewers uninterested in *Seinfeld.*

These strategic uses of violent programs all contradict the frequent claims that violence is not used to attract viewers.

2. *Violence on television is a reflection of violence in society.* Analyzing data across the country on local news content, I found that the percentage of stories devoted to crime and the percentage of lead stories dealing with crime were not related to the crime rate in a city. Rather it was audience interest in crime, reflected by ratings for *Cops* in the market, that predicted the degree local news directors focused on crime in their newscasts. The stronger the audience interest in reality police show programming, the more likely newscasts in an area were to focus on crime.

3. *Images on television do not influence behavior.* Social science research indicates that violent images are more likely to be imitated if they go unpunished, show little pain or suffering, and involve attractive perpetrators. This describes the types of violence often used on television. (For statistical evidence on the context of violence in television, see the work by the National Television Violence Study researchers in *Television Violence and Public Policy,* James T. Hamilton, editor).

4. *Television is less violent today.* It is true that on primetime network broadcast television, the percentage of programs in violent genres has dropped in the 1990s. In 1984 51%

> *"Violent images are more likely to be imitated if they go unpunished, show little pain or suffering, and involve attractive perpetrators."*

of primetime network series were in violent genres, a figure that declined to 23% in 1993. But violence has simply migrated to basic and premium cable channels. Nearly two thirds of all basic cable movies on at 8 P.M. on weekdays are violent. Of the top 5 programs viewed each week on premium channels, over half are violent movies.

5. *What about* Schindler's List? Violence is used in high-quality films. Yet these

types of movies are only a small percentage of those shown on television. In a sample of 5,000 violent movies on broadcast, basic cable, and premium channels, I found that only 3% were given four stars (the highest rating) by critics.

Violence on Television Is a Pollution Problem

In opinion surveys about television, the majority of adult respondents indicates that there is too much violence in entertainment programming. Yet there are segments of viewers who enjoy and consume violent shows. Males age 18–34 are the top consumers of violent entertainment fare, followed by females 18–34. These viewers are particularly prized by advertisers, in part because their purchase decisions can be more easily influenced than those of older consumers. As a result, programmers often target these young adults and use violent shows to attract them. These same violent programs may also attract an unintended audience, children 2–11 and teens 12–17. Primetime shows do not get higher ad rates for attracting child viewers, since the products on these programs are aimed at adults. Yet because the programs are on when children are in the viewing audience (nearly 1 out of 3 children and teens are watching television at 8 P.M. on weekdays), children see violent shows aimed at adults.

This exposure of children to violent programs generates a pollution problem. Research indicates that some children who consume violent programming are more likely to become aggressive, to feel desensitized to violence, or experience fear upon viewing. While the market for violence

> *"Violence is used in high-quality films. Yet these types of movies are only a small percentage of those shown on television."*

works well in delivering a segment of adult viewers what they want, the market fails with respect to shielding children from harmful effects. Neither advertisers nor programmers are led to consider the full costs to society of using violence to attract viewers, since they are not led by the market to internalize in their decision making the negative impacts these programs have on children. The result—too much violence consumed by too many children.

Broadcasters correctly stress that their business is selling audiences to advertisers, not raising or educating children. When they make programming choices, they focus on the number of viewers, the value of these viewers to advertisers, the cost of programs, and the number of competitors offering different types of fare. There are multiple incentives that favor the provision of violent programming by some channels. Violent shows are cheaper for networks to purchase. Violent programs are twice as likely to be exported, which increases the returns to producers. As the number of viewing options increases, channels serving particular niches continue to grow—including those that specialize in developing a brand name for violence. The proliferation of channels will involve an increase in the number of violent viewing options and the intensity of violence on some channels.

If violence on television is a pollution problem, what is to be done? In dealing with everyday pollutants such as toxic chemicals released into the air, the government has a wide array of policy tools to reduce the harms created: zoning of noxious facilities; the direct control of the release of chemicals; the use of liability laws to change behavior; and the taxing of polluting activities. In the media realm the First Amendment rightfully

> *"Neither advertisers nor programmers are led to consider the full costs to society of using violence to attract viewers."*

restricts the policy options available to deal with television violence. However, I do believe that there are at least three steps which industry, encouraged by government, can take to lower the exposure of children: provide accurate content information; consider the likely number of children in the audience when scheduling; and take responsibility for the potential harms that arise from some types of programs.

Parents Need Help in Shielding Their Children

Information Provision. Parents make the ultimate decisions about whether their children will consume violent content. Yet even for the parents most concerned about shielding their children, the costs in terms of time of finding out what programs contain potentially objectionable content, ascertaining when particular programs are on, and monitoring the viewing of their children are extensive. The V-chip and program ratings provided by the television industry offer the potential to reduce the costs to parents of being responsible parents. The V-chip and ratings system will only work, however, if parents believe the system is credible, informative, and effective.

In my research I found that parents do act if provided with program content information. I found that on primetime broadcast network movies, the Nielsen rating for children 2–11 dropped by about 14% on movies that carried a viewer discretion warning. Since these movies were averaging 1.6 million children 2–11 in their audiences, the drop in viewing translated into approximately 220,000 fewer children in the audience for a movie carrying a warning. The warnings had no impact on ratings for teens or adults. But the warnings did change the willingness of some advertisers to sponsor a program. Once a warning was placed on a violent theatrical film shown on network movies, products likely to experience harm to their brand images by being associated with violence were less likely to advertise on the movie. In particular, products consumed by women, by older viewers, and by families with children were less likely to advertise on a movie once it carried a viewer discretion warning. The number of general product ads on a movie also dropped slightly when the warning was placed. Products aimed at men and younger adults were actually more willing to advertise on these movies with warnings, since their consumers report they are less likely to see television violence as a problem. The companies advertising on movies with warnings were those at less risk for brand name damage.

Controversy about content can have a large impact on advertisers. I found that in its first season, ads on *NYPD Blue* sold at a 45% discount because of the initial unwillingness of advertisers to be associated with the program. Broadcasters are reluctant to provide viewers with content information in part because of the fear that this will generate controversy and change the willingness of advertisers to support a particular program. Cable channels have historically provided much more detailed content descriptors for their programs, in part because they are less dependent on advertiser reactions. During the early implementation of the television rating system, I found evidence that continued concern for advertiser reactions kept the broadcast networks from providing accurate program indicators on more controversial programs. Comparing the ratings provided by the networks with program evaluations from the Parents' Television Council, I found that the networks frequently "underlabeled" programs, such as giving a program found by the parents' viewing group to contain "gratuitous sex, explicit dialogue, violent content, or obscene language" a TV-PG rating rather than a TV-14 rating. The networks were more likely to underlabel the programs with higher ad rates. Among the networks, NBC had the highest ad rates on underlabeled programs.

More recent research by Dale Kunkel and colleagues (*An Assessment of the Television Industry's Use of V-chip Ratings*) indicates that over three-fourths of programs with violence did not carry a violence indicator. An obvious first step that industry officials can take to reduce the exposure of children to violent content is to label such content more frequently, though they may be reluctant to do this because of fears of advertiser backlash. The impact of improved labeling will take time to develop, since the current rating system is akin to the provision of software without hardware. As sets with V-chips arrive in the market, parents will be able to use the content rating systems more easily.

> *"Violent shows are cheaper for networks to purchase."*

Industry Officials Must Be More Responsible

Scheduling. A second measure that industry officials could take would be to shift violent programming to times when children are less likely to be in the audience. This would require a substantial change in behavior by some programmers, since the times when children and teens are in the audience are often the same times when viewers 18–34 are in the audience. At 8 P.M. on weekdays, for example, nearly one out of three children and teens is watching television. At this time, nearly two thirds of all movies on basic cable are violent. Fox, which broadcast the highest percentage of violent films among the major networks, often began its movies at 8 P.M. Early evening and daytime hours on weekends are also a frequent time period for the programming of syndicated violent shows. Half of the weekly exposures of children 2–11 to syndicated action adventure/crime series occurs on weekends during the day or early evening before 8 P.M. If programmers were to shift violent content to hours where viewing by children was less likely to arise, this would reduce the probability that those most susceptible to harm were exposed to violent content.

> *"An obvious first step that industry officials can take to reduce the exposure of children to violent content is to label such content more frequently."*

Responsibility. A final measure that industry officials could adopt is to admit that some programs may be damaging for some children to watch. In debates about television violence, executives often deny the potential for harm to arise from programming. Parents will be more likely to act to shield their children from violent programming if there is a more consistent message about likely dangers. I found that parents who were personally bothered by television violence were much more likely to intervene and switch channels when objectionable content came on while children were viewing. Parent groups, educators, pediatricians, and foundations all have a role in alerting parents to the need to shield children from violent content and providing information on how to use options such as the ratings system and V-chip. Entertainment officials also have a role to play in this education process. The targeting and repetition of messages to change consumer decisions is the economic foundation of television programming. If the industry could add an additional message to the information it conveys, that violent content may be harmful and parents should shield their children from it, there may be a high pay off to society from this type of advertising.

News Coverage of Crime Contributes to the Problem of Media Violence

by Derrick Z. Jackson

About the author: *Derrick Z. Jackson is a contributing columnist for* Liberal Opinion Week.

At a May 13, 1999, Senate hearing on violent youth entertainment, Kansas Republican Sam Brownback railed against "movies that depict teens killing their classmates; music with lyrics that glorify suicide, torture, and murder; TV that trivializes the consequences of violence; and video games that simulate real-life killing and give points for each death."

Utah's Orrin Hatch and Connecticut's Joseph Lieberman raised the idea of a federal probe into the marketing of violent video games, movies, and music. Lieberman said that senators do not want to resort to regulation, but if the entertainment industry "continues to market death and degradation to our children, and continues to pay no heed to the genuine bloodshed staining our communities, then one way or the other, the government will act."

Former Education Secretary William Bennett showed clips of violent movies that made some in the audience turn their heads. After the second clip, Bennett asked: "Had enough?"

Have we "had enough" of the marketing of death? I doubt it, since meaningful gun control is still way off the table on Capitol Hill. I also doubt it because while the question is being asked with refreshing force about our fantasies and fiction, Littleton has not yet sparked a simultaneous tossing and turning in the medium that we get our real information from: The news.

"If It Bleeds, It Leads"

In our family, we turned off the local TV news a decade ago. We refused to be prisoners to "If it bleeds, it leads." This is humorous to television executives, but it has led to a horrible distortion of the world we present to our families.

A 1997 study by the University of Miami of local TV news in New York, Los Angeles, Chicago, Miami, Indianapolis, Austin, Texas, Syracuse, New York, and Eugene, Oregon found that 29 percent of newscasts were about crime. A study last year found that 33 percent of local TV news in Baltimore and Philadelphia was on crime.

Crime received twice as much coverage than politics in the Miami study and 14 times more than education and 24 times more than race relations. Of course, as a 1994 study of Chicago TV news found, news executives degrade race relations by disproportionately singling out black criminals.

> *Less than one-half of 1 percent of youths . . . were arrested for violent crimes in 1994, [but] 55 percent of the television news stories on youths involved violence.*"

Princell Hair, news director at the NBC affiliate in Baltimore, said stations sometimes purposely tie a real murder story to lead the late-night news right after movies on the Mafia and shows like "Homicide." "Whenever we have the opportunity to tie into a preceding program, we try to take advantage of it," Hair said.

In doing so, the news media cross the line into a ratings game that, no less than a video game, gets points for every death. "What television seems to cultivate is what we call the 'mean-world syndrome,' said longtime media analyst George Gerbner of the Annenberg School of Communication at the University of Pennsylvania. "If you're growing up in a heavy-viewing home, for all practical purposes, you live in a meaner world."

There is plenty of evidence that constant exposure to mean worlds creates meaner people, whether we are talking about aggression after watching "Power Rangers" or the rise of crime among nations and groups of people as they watched more television.

Distorting Reality

There is so much evidence that there is no longer any excuse to present news as one-third crime. Crime rates have fallen in most cities. There is no excuse to report on violence with no context. A 1997 study of 26 California TV stations found that 84 percent of stories on violence covered just the act, but no factors that led to or could have prevented the crime.

Every one is angry about how innocence was stolen at Columbine High. TV news steals innocence every night. The California study found that even though less than one-half of 1 percent of youths 10 to 17 years old were arrested for violent crimes in 1994, 55 percent of the television news stories on youths involved violence.

It is no wonder, then, that despite the highly publicized national drop in violent crime, a Gallup poll last fall showed that 56 percent of Americans felt there was more crime than five years ago, compared to 35 percent who felt there was less.

Had enough? The answer will be yes when Americans reject the distorted reality that passes as news; when we reject not only the quantity of stories about violence but also photos of dead bodies that do not add to stories; and when we stop stripping people of their dignity. Do we need to see mothers in primal screams at death scenes? Do we need to hear every 911 call?

The answer will be yes when we reject "news" that becomes wallet photos for gang members and Trenchcoat wannabes. The answer will be yes when we stop feeding on a fear and paranoia that focuses us more on revenge and the death penalty than the prevention of gun control. Had enough? We can prove it by sending the news makers a loud and clear message. Click.

Violence in the Media Contributes to the Violence in Society

by Michael Massing

About the author: *Journalist Michael Massing is a contributing editor of the* Columbia Journalism Review *and the author of* The Fix: Solving the Nation's Drug Problem.

At a recent dinner at a friend's house, there was much groaning about Congress's failure to pass a serious gun-control measure. New York liberals all, we bemoaned the gun lobby's ability to triumph once again, even in the wake of the bloodletting in Littleton.

And wasn't it depressing, I added, that, once again, the issue of the media's role as purveyors of violence was probably not going to be addressed in any meaningful way?

Liberal Denials

There was a moment of awkward silence. "You don't really think that violence in the media has anything to do with Littleton, do you?" said a woman sitting across from me.

"I don't see how beating up on Hollywood is going to have any effect on the level of violence in this country," declared a woman to my left.

"People keep talking about violence in the media," a third put in. "Yet the juvenile crime rate is going down."

Hoping for allies, I noted that hundreds of studies have been conducted on the subject of media violence over the past 30 years, and almost without exception they have found a clear link to aggressive behavior, especially among young people. The evidence is so strong, I said, that among most researchers there was no longer any debate.

It was to no avail. Most of those around the table would not be budged from their position that media violence is a fake issue pursued by Republicans for political gain.

I was not surprised. For years, I've been fighting this same battle. My friends' comments have become fairly standard:

"We all grew up watching 'The Three Stooges,' yet we turned out okay." Or, "If parents dislike what's on TV, they should turn off their sets." Or, "Hollywood is simply providing what people want. The market rules."

I understand such sentiments. Once, I even shared them. Years ago, when Tipper Gore proposed putting warning labels on music album covers, I snickered along with a lot of other people. My views began to change, however, when I began researching the drug trade in East Harlem for a book I was writing. In the process, I heard gruesome stories about addicts stabbing one another over grains of heroin, about crackheads throwing children from building rooftops, about teenagers tortured and executed for coming up a few dollars short in a drug deal.

Glamorizing Violence

In the midst of this, I saw "Pulp Fiction." The movie was clever, but given what I was learning about real-life violence, I found it hard to laugh at Quentin Tarantino's breezy "do you know what they call a Quarter Pounder with cheese in Paris" approach to murder and brutality. I was even more put off by the rousing reception the movie got from (mostly liberal) film critics. The film's graphic content, they knowingly insisted, was meant to be taken ironically, as a witty commentary on violence in America. To me, though, the movie—by suggesting that we could be entertained by such acts—seemed to raise our tolerance for them.

Then came "L.A. Confidential." Yes, the movie had an intriguing plot and interesting characters. But in terms of body count, it outdid even "Pulp Fiction." Every important conflict in the film was resolved with weapons or fists, culminating in the preposterously bloody final shootout. None-

> *"Movie violence has become so endemic that it infects even 'family' comedies."*

theless, my liberal friends raved and the critics swooned. "True," Anthony Lane wrote in the *New Yorker,* the movie "glistens with wrongdoing of every stripe— a gashed throat in a motel, a herd of cops on a Christmas rampage, a multiple slaying at the Nite Owl Cafe. There are hookers and hopheads, and some juicy political blackmail. Yet the film itself is oddly delicate, and much of the blood is spilled long before we step in it." Oddly delicate? Gashed throats and multiple slayings?

It could be argued, of course, that "Pulp Fiction" and "L.A. Confidential" were aimed at adult viewers. Yet the movies directed at younger audiences—"The Matrix," the "Lethal Weapon" series, the endless Schwarzenegger, Seagal and

Stallone flicks—seem even more explicitly violent. Movie violence has become so endemic that it infects even "family" comedies such as "Home Alone," in which the hapless Joe Pesci and Daniel Stern are repeatedly thwacked and thwunked. What's worse, these movies are routinely shown on television, along-side Jerry Springer, pro wrestling, "Cops," "911," and all the other variations on the theme. Even the Lifetime cable channel, which aims itself at women, frequently airs movies featuring slashings, stabbings and shootings—only there it's usually the women who commit the violence (in self-defense, of course).

> *"Should we be closing our eyes to the links that studies have found between media violence and aggressive behavior?"*

Can exposure to such programming influence young people to behave violently? The families of the three victims in the 1997 school shooting in West Paducah, Kentucky, think so. They have alleged in a lawsuit that the perpetrator was inspired by "The Basketball Diaries," with its fantasy sequence featuring Leonardo DiCaprio barging into a classroom and riddling his teacher and classmates with bullets. The suit is seeking damages from the film's makers and distributors, including Time Warner and Polygram Film Entertainment Distribution, as well as from the makers of "Mortal Kombat" and other violent video games that the young gunman allegedly played.

Needless to say, other factors were involved in the recent spate of school shootings. And of course, few of the millions of teenagers exposed to violent movies and video games go out and shoot people. Nonetheless, should we be closing our eyes to the links that studies have found between media violence and aggressive behavior? In both 1972 and 1982, the U.S. Surgeon General's office conducted comprehensive overviews of the existing research; both times, it found televised violence contributed to antisocial behavior. Between 1990 and 1996, the American Medical Association, the American Psychological Association, the National Institute of Mental Health, the American Academy of Pediatrics and the American Academy of Child and Adolescent Psychiatry unanimously concluded that TV violence contributed to violence in the real world.

Not Just an Issue for Republicans

Doing something about this would seem a natural cause for liberals, especially those of baby-boom vintage. As parents, baby boomers are known for their obsessive efforts to protect their children—childproofing their homes, finding good books to read to them, hunting for the best schools. Though not a parent myself, I can think of few things more threatening to the psychological well-being of kids than the muck served up by Hollywood. Yet, when it comes to insulating their kids from it, many boomers can't be bothered.

Frank Rich, a *New York Times* columnist and baby-boom oracle, has frequently mocked politicians who express concern over violence in the media. In a June 19, 1999, column, Rich inveighed against politicians who give "hypocritical sermons about pop culture." Among his chief targets: Republican William Bennett, the former secretary of education who has made a name for himself through his books about values and moral decline. "The bodies had hardly been buried in Littleton," Rich wrote, "when Mr. Virtue took to the pulpit of 'Meet the Press' to target 'the Levins, the Bronfmans, the people who run Viacom' for spewing cultural rot." In testimony before Congress, Rich said, Bennett singled out "the Edgar Bronfmans, Howard Stringers, Michael Eisners and Oliver Stones." Missing from the list, Rich gleefully pointed out, was "Republican fat cat" Rupert Murdoch, whose Twentieth Century Fox movie studio is bringing out the violent "Fight Club.". . .

Because Rich is so intent on deriding the Republican Bennett, he can't seem to see that the purveyors of violence transcend ideological categories—that they come from both political parties and include fat cats on the left and the right. Rich's narrow-minded analysis helps explain why liberals are so reluctant to take on media violence. The issue has traditionally been pushed by conservatives, and their pronouncements often seem part of a broader moral crusade. Certainly some conservatives are so motivated. But just because Bill Bennett has embraced an issue seems an insufficient reason to dismiss it. In fact, reining in media violence would seem to dovetail with many liberal causes, such as stricter gun control, more affordable child care, and expanded after-school programs.

> *"Political officials need to speak out loudly and repeatedly about the irresponsible practices of movie and TV executives."*

Another, more serious concern is the specter of government involvement. In his column, Rich excoriated Representative Henry Hyde (R-Illinois) for introducing a bill to prohibit the sale of "obscenely" sexual and violent material to minors under the age of 17. This objection is well-founded; no supporter of the First Amendment can rest easy at the thought of Congress regulating the content of movies or TV programs.

Shaming Hollywood and the TV Industry

So what is to be done? The government does have a role to play in combating media violence—but not by passing laws. Without tampering with the First Amendment, political officials need to speak out loudly and repeatedly about the irresponsible practices of movie and TV executives.

Of course, some politicians have done this. In the wake of Littleton, for instance, President Clinton has criticized the excesses of the movie industry. Unfortunately, his close ties to Hollywood have kept his message muted, as can be seen from his lame proposal to conduct an 18-month study to determine whether entertainment companies deliberately market violence to kids. A quick glance at a calendar shows that an 18-month deadline means the study won't be ready until the 2000 election is over, which means the Clinton administration won't have to act on it. Hollywood—and Al Gore's fund-raisers—breathed a collective sigh of relief.

> *"If enough voices are raised, Sony and Viacom and Fox would find it in their corporate interest to eliminate. . . objectionable and gratuitous scenes from their products."*

President Clinton's other contribution to the debate—the V-chip—seems no more promising. The technology, which must be incorporated into all TV sets larger than 13 inches after January 1, 2000, is designed to block out violent and sexually explicit TV shows. In championing the law back in 1996, Clinton said it puts the remote back into the hands of parents. But in placing the burden on Mom and Dad, the V-chip takes it off the place it most belongs: Hollywood.

What we need is a concerted and sustained campaign designed to shame the Levins, Bronfmans and, yes, the Murdochs into behaving like responsible citizens. Could such an approach work? It has with the tobacco industry. Not long ago, the cigarette companies seemed invincible. But then the American people elected a president who was willing to take them on, especially on the issue of marketing to kids, and eventually the industry was forced to reform. The same could happen with the entertainment world. If enough voices are raised, Sony and Viacom and Fox would find it in their corporate interest to eliminate—voluntarily—objectionable and gratuitous scenes from their products.

Bringing this about, however, will take strong leadership from the White House. It also will take vocal participation by liberals. Otherwise, Hollywood can easily reject a jawboning campaign as driven by partisanship. And who better to get to the liberals who dominate Hollywood than their fellow liberals? Imagine if at next year's Academy Awards, activists such as Alec Baldwin began talking not about Tibet but about the mindless violence being served up on the big screen. If that happened, things might change very quickly. It might even make for a good movie with a classic Hollywood theme, in which a few brave souls battle, and defeat, an all-powerful adversary. Sylvester Stallone could even play the lead.

The Problem of Media Violence Does Not Justify Censorship

by Joan E. Bertin

About the author: *Joan E. Bertin is executive director of the National Coalition Against Censorship, an alliance of organizations that work to defend the First Amendment right of free speech.*

Good morning. My name is Joan Bertin. I am the Executive Director of the National Coalition Against Censorship ("NCAC"). NCAC is an alliance of 48 national non-profit organizations, including religious, educational, professional, labor and civil rights groups, united in their support for freedom of thought, inquiry, and expression. NCAC educates the public and policy makers about threats to free expression, mobilizes grass roots support for the First Amendment, provides advice and assistance to individuals engaged in debates about censorship, and advocates for laws and decisions protective of free speech and democratic values.

Thank you for this opportunity to address the Task Force on Youth Violence and the Entertainment Industry. My testimony today will discuss the implications of the First Amendment for proposals to rate and restrict video games and other entertainment for violent content.

The Allure of Censorship

Before I reach the constitutional issues, however, I want to start with a brief discussion of censorship in general. It comes as a surprise to most people that censorship is a significant, if under-recognized, problem. We receive hundreds of inquiries each year about censorship controversies around the country, including many in New York State. For every call we receive, there are many instances of censorship that we don't hear about, and other instances in which self-censorship disguises, but does not resolve, the problem.

Joan E. Bertin's testimony before the New York State Task Force on Youth Violence and the Entertainment Industry, October 6, 1999, Albany, NY. Reprinted with permission. Testimony available at www.ncac.org.

Every year, we receive complaints about books like *The Adventures of Huckleberry Finn, Of Mice and Men, Scary Stories to Tell in the Dark, Blubber,* and more. Complaints relate to every conceivable subject matter: sex, religion, violence, racial themes, multiculturalism, bullying, insolence, evolution, witchcraft, cursing, too realistic, too unrealistic, and so on. In short, the impulse to censor is alive and well, and almost everything is vulnerable to challenge.

As this indicates, sensibilities about art and literature vary widely, as do views on what is appropriate for children to see and hear. The First Amendment accounts for these different perspectives through its core principle which allows each of us to decide for ourselves what to read, see, say, hear, and think. Once we depart from this principle, however, it would become difficult or impossible to limit the exception to certain issues, venues or forms of expression. If an exception is made for violent content, why not for the sacrilegious, or subversive? If in video games, why not films and television?

Like almost all First Amendment advocates, I am concerned about violence. I'm the mother of two teenagers, so I also have all the concerns of most parents about school safety and safety on the street. But, at the same time, I also believe that my children benefit greatly from living in a country where they are allowed to read widely, to express themselves freely, and to think independently. And I, like most parents, oppose governmental interference in my judgments and decisions about my entertainment choices and child-rearing philosophy.

The First Amendment Protects Violent Speech

Turning now to the issue of governmental efforts to regulate violent content in certain forms of entertainment, unlike the situation with obscenity, the Supreme Court has never carved out an exception in First Amendment analysis for violent speech and images. This is true, even where minors are concerned. In the more extreme case involving speech that advocates violence, the Court has refused to penalize it unless it constitutes actual incitement to lawless action. You may recall the case *NAACP v. Claiborne Hardware,* (1982), which involved a boycott of white merchants organized by the National Association for the Advancement of Colored People, involving speech advocating violence, threats of violence, and some actual violence. Nonetheless, the Court held that "mere advocacy of the use of force or violence does not remove speech from the protection of the

> *"The impulse to censor is alive and well."*

First Amendment." This and numerous other cases demonstrate that real life violent speech is protected under the First Amendment in circumstances where the threat to public safety and order is palpable, although not imminent.

The Court has also specifically considered violence in popular entertainment. As long ago as 1948, *Winters v. New York,* established that such material is fully protected by the First Amendment, *regardless of its social worth.* The statute at issue made it a crime to print, publish, or disseminate "criminal news, police reports, or accounts of criminal deeds, or pictures, or stories of deeds of bloodshed, lust, or crime." The statute was defended on the ground that the material would incite violence and that it was within the "state's police power to minimize all incentives to crime, particularly in the field of sanguinary or salacious publications with their stimulation of juvenile delinquency." The Court observed that it "can see nothing of any possible value to society in these magazines," but nonetheless found that "they are as much entitled to the protection of free speech as the best of literature."

> *"The Supreme Court has never carved out an exception in First Amendment analysis for violent speech and images. This is true, even where minors are concerned."*

Although the opportunity has presented itself on several occasions since then, the Court has consistently declined to depart from this rule, or to treat violent content as an exception to the First Amendment, as it has done in its analysis of sexually explicit obscene materials. Lower court decisions have followed suit. For example, in *Video Software Dealers Association v. Webster,* (1992) the Eighth Circuit Court of Appeals struck down a statute restricting the sale or rental of violent films to minors, and in *Eclipse Enterprises, Inc. v. Gulotta,* (1997) the Second Circuit held unconstitutional an ordinance forbidding the sale of "heinous crime" trading cards to minors. (Of course, First Amendment restrictions on censorship of violent content by government officials do not apply to private individuals or organizations providing information to consumers about the content of entertainment products, or voicing opinions about their quality and other characteristics. These actions sometimes result in a form of censorship, but the First Amendment does not reach it.)

Video games provide an easy target because they are often characterized as entertainment with little social value. In *Winters,* however, the Court rejected the claim that First Amendment protections apply only to "worthy" material or to "the exposition of ideas," and stated instead that the "line between the informing and the entertaining is too elusive for the protection of that basic right." More recently, the Supreme Court has relied on *Winters* and other cases to observe that First Amendment guarantees are "'not confined to the expression of ideas that are conventional or shared by a majority.'. . . Nor is it relevant that [such] materials . . . are arguably devoid of any ideological content. The line between the transmission of ideas and mere entertainment is much too elusive for this Court to draw, if indeed such a line can be drawn at all." (*Stanley v. Georgia,* 1969)

No doubt, the High Court's reservations about carving out an exception in First Amendment jurisprudence for violence stem at least in part from a recognition that doing so would threaten a wide range of artistic and political expression. If the First Amendment did not fully protect violent imagery and graphic descriptions, a great deal of literature, art, media, and other material would be vulnerable to censorship, depending on the sensibilities of the moment and individuals charged with making the determination. For example, graphic depictions of violence can be found in the Bible, *The Odyssey, Agamemnon,* Faulkner's *Light in August,* and James Dickey's *Deliverance;* in films such as *Paths of Glory, The Seventh Seal,* and *The Godfather;* in Picasso's *Guernica* and almost all religious art depicting the Crucifixion and religious martyrdom; and in theater including much of Shakespeare (*Macbeth, Henry V, Titus Andronicus*).

A Part of Human Nature

Violence has always been a feature of popular entertainment as well as more high-brow fare. *The Punch and Judy Show* depicted domestic and child abuse, among other things, and Paris's Grand Guignol Theater's horror shows included scenes of hands being cut off at the wrist and the flesh being cut off a young girl. It is difficult to imagine anything more violent that the Roman Circus or public executions, which were a form of mass entertainment in some times and places. In our day, the wrestling match and the evening news provide an ample dose of violent content. The horrific image of a napalmed child is certainly seared into the memories of many of us.

Critics assail unrealistic depictions of violence in movies like *Pulp Fiction,* and even *Tom & Jerry* cartoons, because they are said to "trivialize" violence or "desensitize" viewers to its effects. But, as noted, the History Channel, many news shows, and some sporting events, all offer nightmarish images, bad role models, and examples of wrong-doing going unpunished. If anything, it's reality that numbs our senses, not fiction.

Popular culture has often been the particular target of censorship campaigns. In the 19th century, popular novels were attacked as a corrupting influence, as were comic books in the mid-20th century. It is worth remembering that entertainment once attacked as low-class and corrupting sometimes comes into the mainstream and is even given value by later generations. Mozart's *Marriage of Figaro* was once considered "low class" entertainment, as were Shakespeare's comedies. Even material that will never rise to such exalted heights merits recognition as entertainment and an outlet for human emotion. Whether video games will ever be culturally redeemed as worthy entertainment remains to be seen. The fact is that adults purchase most video games, that millions of people enjoy them as a form of entertainment, and that few (if any) are inspired by them to engage in violent criminal activity.

> *"[Violence in popular entertainment] is fully protected by the First Amendment, regardless of its social worth."*

If that were the standard for censorship, however, almost nothing would be safe. If we regulated the things that violent criminals have cited as their inspiration, we would have to restrict the Bible, among many other great works of art and literature. The fact that someone cites the Bible or the Koran or anything else in an effort to justify violence does not require that we take the claim seriously, or consider it exculpatory, or decide that the thing should be censored. To implicitly cede to violent criminals the power to define for the entire community what ideas and images are "dangerous" is to put the inmates in charge of the asylum.

We are a violent species, and were long before video games or any other forms of modern electronic media could be blamed—think of the Crusades, the Inquisition, the Holocaust and other institutionalized forms of torture and violence. The most stunning examples of violence in our own time do not bear even a remote link to video games or any form of media violence: the ferocious nationalistic and tribal violence in Kosovo, Rwanda, and Somalia; sanctioned penalties, like stoning, imposed in some places for individuals convicted of adultery or pre-marital sex; butchered bodies in a mass grave in East Timor; or, closer to home, middle-aged white men venting incomprehensible anger by shooting randomly into a brokerage house and church full of teenagers. The vast majority of violent acts have nothing whatsoever to do with media violence or any other single feature of modern society. Human behavior is more complicated than that.

Just this point was made in the National Research Council's report on *Understanding and Preventing Violence* (1993):

> The likelihood of someone's committing a violent act depends on many factors. Biological, individual, family, peer, school, and community factors may influence the development of an individual potential for violence. Whether the potential becomes manifest as a violent act depends on the interactions between this violence potential and immediate situational factors, such as the consumption of alcohol and the presence of a victim. . . . [N]o one influence in isolation is likely to account for the development of a potential for violence, except perhaps in some special cases. It is possible that to produce a violent adult, one needs, at a minimum, a child born with a particular temperamental profile, living in a particular family constellation, in a disadvantaged neighborhood, exposed to models of aggression and patterns of reinforcement of aggressive behavior, having a particular school experience, having a particular set of peer relations, and also experiencing certain chance events that permit the actualization of violent behavior. . . .

Recent crime statistics, indicating a decline in violent crimes in the society at large and in schools during the very time period that media critics cite a rise in violence in the media, further undermine claims of a causal relationship between media violence and criminal acts.

The Wrong Response

To paraphrase H.L. Mencken, for every complex problem there is a simple solution, and it is almost always wrong. Regulating violent content in video games or other forms of entertainment is the wrong response to a complex problem. Whatever one thinks of video games, we all have a stake in preserving the right to read, see, hear, and think as we choose without government interference. Regulation of violent content in one arena invites it in all, as the Supreme Court observed in *Winters v. New York:* "The present case . . . involves the circulation of only vulgar magazines. The next may call for a decision as to free expression of political views. . . ." It is impossible to distinguish rationally and consistently between "acceptable" and "unacceptable" violent content. That judgment is inherently subjective. The Constitution accordingly allows each of us to make our own decisions about such content, gives parents the right to set their own guidelines for their minor children, and restricts the role of government in controlling these choices.

> *"Graphic depictions of violence can be found in the Bible,* **The Odyssey,** **Agamemnon,** *Faulkner's* **Light in August,** *and James Dickey's* **Deliverance."**

If the premise is that it is constitutionally permissible to infringe the rights of all, in an effort to control the behavior of a few, a less constitutionally vulnerable option is stricter regulation of firearms. This would be less vulnerable to constitutional challenge because, unlike violent media, firearms are the "but for" cause of much violent crime, and restrictions on access to weapons would unquestionably be more effective in reducing violent crime than restrictions on access to violent media. Thus, if violence prevention is sufficiently compelling to warrant an infringement of constitutional rights, there is a sounder basis for regulating gun ownership, because of the clear correlation between firearms and violence. In contrast, if concerns about the Second Amendment rights of law-abiding individuals are thought to preclude such an approach, then it should be a foregone conclusion that it is unacceptable to impose limitations on the First Amendment rights of similarly law-abiding individuals.

Recent case law in the Second Circuit should also give pause to legislative efforts to regulate violent content. In *Eclipse Enterprises, Inc. v. Gulotta,* (1997), the Second Circuit Court of Appeals held that the effort to regulate "heinous crime" trading cards was content-based because of its focus on violence, and that it was presumptively invalid absent a showing that the regulation satisfied the "strict scrutiny" test. That test requires proof that the regulation serves a compelling governmental interest, that it is necessary to achieve that interest, and that it is narrowly tailored. In this case, the test was not satisfied. The court found that there was no research demonstrating a link between the cards and juvenile crime, that studies of television violence were inconclusive and inapplicable, and that no reason had been advanced why this particular form of entertainment was singled out for regulation. The court concluded that the "First Amendment imposes a high standard of precision on legislative efforts to regulate content-based speech, and the law under scrutiny here simply does not meet that standard." Virtually all federal courts to consider the question of government regulation of violent speech or expression are in agreement with the Second Circuit. It is no accident that efforts to justify such regulations have failed, given the significant infringement on First Amendment interests involved, and the hypothetical and conjectural nature of the claims of causality.

Only an Emergency Can Justify Suppression of Speech

The "bedrock principle underlying the First Amendment . . . is that the government may not prohibit the expression of an idea simply because society finds the idea itself offensive or disagreeable" (*Texas v. Johnson,* 1989). At bottom, efforts to restrict and regulate violent content in various media are just that—efforts to suppress the offensive and disagreeable. Long ago [in *Whitney v. California,* 274 U.S. 357, 376-8 (1927)], Justice Brandeis wisely observed:

> Fear of serious injury cannot alone justify suppression of free speech and assembly. Men feared witches and burnt women. It is the function of speech to free men from the bondage of irrational fears. To justify suppression of free speech there must be reasonable ground to fear that serious evil will result if free speech is practiced. There must be reasonable ground to believe that the danger apprehended is imminent. . . .

> [N]o danger flowing from speech can be deemed clear and present, unless the incidence of the evil apprehended is so imminent that it may befall before there is opportunity for full discussion. If there be time to expose through discussion the falsehood and fallacies, to avert the evil by the processes of education, the remedy to be applied is more speech, not enforced silence. Only an emergency can justify repression. Such must be the rule if authority is to be reconciled with freedom. Such, in my opinion, is the command of the Constitution. It is therefore always open to Americans to challenge a law abridging free speech and assembly by showing that there was no emergency justifying it. . . .

> Among free men, the deterrents ordinarily to be applied to prevent crime are education and punishment for violations of the law, not abridgment of the rights of free speech and assembly.

I urge you to address violence in ways that are respectful of free speech and expression rights. Not only are the traditions and lessons of the First Amendment worthy of such respect, but taking the focus off suppressing expression, and placing it squarely on preventing violent conduct, is undoubtedly a more effective way to reduce crime than giving government the power to legislate about the content or quality of entertainment.

Guns Are a More Serious Problem than Media Violence

by Barry Glassner

About the author: *Barry Glassner is a professor of sociology at the University of Southern California and the author of* The Culture of Fear: Why Americans Are Afraid of the Wrong Things.

Some American reporters and editors have swallowed so much baloney fed to them by the gun lobby they cough up explanations for gun deaths that credit everything *except* guns. They even blame their own industry. A columnist in *Newsweek* wrote of the Dunblane massacre [in which a man gunned down sixteen elementary school children in Dunblane, Scotland], "Onanistic solitude, lived out in a fantasy world ruled by terror and thrilled by incessant gunfire, poses a lethal combination. Media moguls, enriched by promoting these fantasies, deny any blame for society's degradation. They are only giving society what it demands, they say."

Blame It on the Tube

In other words, it is the guns on TV that cause people to die in real life. Numerous American journalists, including some of the most intelligent among them, have actively endorsed the dizzy proposition that television creates "a reality of its own that may crowd out our real reality," as Daniel Schorr, a network news correspondent for twenty-nine years before he moved to National Public Radio, put it. In an essay in the *Christian Science Monitor* Schorr gave as a case example John Hinckley, who "spent many hours alone in a room with a TV set, retreating into a world of fantasy violence" before his attempted assassination of President Ronald Reagan. Interviewed by the Secret Service after the shooting, his first question was, "Is it on TV?" Schorr also rehearsed familiar statistics about the average eighteen-year-old having witnessed 200,000 acts of violence, including 40,000 murders, on the tube. At these levels of exposure, Schorr contended, young people "no longer know the difference between the bang-bang they grow up with on the television screen and the bang-bang that snuffs out real lives."

He may be right, but some of the historical antecedents of this line of reasoning are worth noting. During the golden age of radio scholars produced studies showing that listening impaired young people's capacity to distinguish reality from fantasy. And centuries earlier Plato cautioned against those who would tell stories to youngsters. "Children cannot distinguish between what is allegory and what isn't," says Socrates in Plato's *Republic*, "and opinions formed at that age are difficult to change."

That society survived both the radio and the scroll should be of some reassurance. So should a recent study from UCLA's Center for Communication Policy, which carefully analyzed 3,000 hours of TV programming on the major networks in the mid-1990s. The study found that a large proportion of the most sinister and decontextualized acts of violence on TV appear in cartoon shows such as "Batman and Robin" and on goofy prime-time programs such as "America's Funniest Home Videos," neither of which is likely to be confused with real life. By contrast, some of the most homicidal shows, such as "NYPD Blue" and "Homicide," portrayed violence as horribly painful and destructive and not to be treated lightly.

Questioning the Research on Media Violence

In a discerning op-ed piece in the *New York Times* author Patrick Cooke made a parallel observation: If young Americans have seen tens of thousands of murders on TV, surely, he commented, they have seen even more acts of kindness. On sitcoms, romantic comedies, movies of the week, soaps, medical dramas, and even on police shows, people are constantly falling in love and helping each other out. The characters on most prime-time shows "share so much peace, tolerance and understanding that you might even call it gratuitous harmony," Cooke observes. Why not conclude, he asks, that TV encourages niceness at least as much as it encourages violence?

Yet social scientists who study relationships between TV violence and real-world violence, and whose research journalists, politicians, and activists cite in fear mongering about crime on TV, do not make niceness one of their outcome measures. They also neglect to pursue some important cross-cultural comparisons.

> *"If young Americans have seen tens of thousands of murders on TV, surely, . . . they have seen even more acts of kindness."*

Some of the most seemingly persuasive studies relate what people watched as children to how aggressive or violent they are as adults. A heavy diet of TV brutality early in life correlates with violent behavior later on, the researchers demonstrate. Whether these correlations truly prove that TV violence provokes actual violence has been questioned, however, by social scientists who propose as a counterhypothesis that people already predisposed to violence are particularly attracted to violent TV programs. Equally important, when researchers outside the United States try to replicate these studies they come up empty-handed. Researchers in several countries find no relationship between adults' levels of violence and the amount of TV violence they watched as kids.

> *"TV shows do not kill or maim people. Guns do."*

One widely quoted researcher who has made cross-national comparisons is Brandon Centerwall, a professor of psychiatry at the University of Washington, who has estimated that there would be 10,000 fewer murders each year in the United States and 700,000 fewer assaults had TV never been invented. Centerwall based these numbers on an analysis of crime rates before and after the introduction of television in particular towns in Canada and South Africa. But what about present-time comparisons? David Horowitz, head of the Center for the Study of Popular Culture, a conservative advocacy organization, correctly points out that viewers in Detroit, Michigan, see the same TV shows as viewers in Windsor, Ontario, just across the river. Yet the murder rate in Detroit has been thirty times that in Windsor.

Guns Are the Real Problem

TV shows do not kill or maim people. Guns do. It is the unregulated possession of guns, more than any other factor, that accounts for the disparity in fatality rates from violent crime in the United States compared to most of the world. The inadequate control of guns often accounts for the loss of life in dramatic crime incidents outside the United States as well—the massacre in Dunblane, Scotland, being a case in point. A difference between there and here, however, is that they accept the point and act on it. After the Dunblane tragedy the House of Commons strengthened Britain's already ardent gun laws by outlawing all handguns larger than .22 caliber.

Violence in the Media Reflects the Violence in Society

by Katha Pollitt

About the author: *Katha Pollitt is a columnist for the* Nation, *an independent weekly opinion magazine.*

It didn't take long for the press to connect 21-year-old white-supremacist multikiller Benjamin Smith with the all-purpose explanation du jour: violent entertainment, in this case the computer game Dungeons & Dragons. This replaces the explanation, given by his mentor, Matt Hale, leader of the World Church of the Creator, that Smith was driven to shoot minorities in the Midwest over the July 4, 1999, weekend—six Orthodox Jews, at least three blacks, two Asians—because political correctness prevented him from expressing his racial theories verbally. It turns out Smith expressed himself verbally quite a bit: His views were widely known to his fellow students at Indiana University. And physically, too: He had been forced to withdraw from the University of Illinois after beating up a girlfriend in the dorm. As with the Littleton killers, there were plenty of warning signs. One neighbor from Wilmette, Illinois, where the Smith family lived during Benjamin's teen years, said she was afraid of him and was relieved when he moved away.

Of course, even if Dungeons & Dragons had totally warped Smith's mind, which I doubt, you can't kill many people driving around with a virtual sword. For that you need guns. In the wake of Littleton, it looked for a moment there as if Congress would be shamed into at least token gun-control legislation, but in the end John Dingell—a Democrat, for those of you who still like to blame the Republicans for all our woes—saved the nation from the dreadful prospect of having to wait for a background check before buying a personal arsenal from an unlicensed dealer at a gun show. The kind of serious, comprehensive legislation it would take to make a significant dent in the easy availability of firearms—a feature unique to the United States among Western industrialized nations—is decades, maybe lifetimes away.

So forget gun control. Media violence is the trendy cause now. In the *Washington Post,* Michael Massing declares it's beyond question that the media are connected to real-world violence, although I find it hard to believe that the movies he singles out—*LA Confidential* and *Pulp Fiction*—had anything to do with the inner-city violence that he says shaped his views: crackheads throwing children off rooftops, teens killed in penny ante drug deals (besides, isn't rap music the usual suspect here?). Still, you won't find me defending art films loaded with stylized killing, hyperviolent action films, super-gory horror flicks, misogynous heavy metal and rap, violent computer games, slap-happy cartoons, sadomasochistic fashion spreads or sexist music videos. Whether or not you can connect this cultural effluvia to specific acts of violence in a one-to-one causal way, thousands of hours of it can't be good for the soul.

Americans Enjoy Violent Entertainment

But realistically, what does one do with that insight beyond curling up with a good book? The government is not about to censor pop culture, a huge commercial enterprise, any more than it's about to enact real checks on guns, another huge commercial enterprise. And there's another problem with fighting media violence. You wouldn't know this from the way the issue is presented by proponents of media uplift, but most Americans don't disapprove of the current media fare—they love it! The anti-slash-and-sleaze constituency is small and getting smaller. According to a recent Associated Press poll taken during the post-Littleton debate over media violence, only one-third of Americans said violence is the biggest problem with current movies. (The same number cited ticket prices.) And the 40 percent who said violence would make them less likely to see a film is down from the 60 percent who gave that answer a decade ago. Moreover, most of those in that 40 percent are women, old people and people who hardly ever go to the movies.

It skews the issue to present the problem as one of "youth culture"—worried, disapproving parents falling asleep over Preston Sturges reruns while their crazy kids watch *Natural Born Killers* with one eye and update their racist Web site with the other. Much of America is deeply fascinated by violent entertainment. The whole family watches *COPS* and *NYPD Blue* and *Homicide,* and idolizes athletes, musicians and actors with records of brutality against women. Massing mentions *Home Alone,* which struck me too as containing rather a lot of supposedly humorous physical cruelty for a movie aimed at small children. But so what? *Home Alone* was the eleventh biggest-grossing movie ever.

> *"Much of America is deeply fascinated by violent entertainment."*

Or take wrestling. It's violent, racist, sexist and witless—Americans can't get enough of it, and now their kids can't either. Recently, a 7-year-old in Dallas killed his 3-year-old brother when he demonstrated a wrestling move he'd seen on TV—a pretty clear demonstration of a connection between media violence and the real thing—but how far do you think a campaign to confine televised wrestling to the post-bedtime hours would get? The idea that Americans have been imposed upon by entertainment moguls who have seized control of culture is much too simple. That's why Massing's proposal that "we" shame Hollywood into cleaning up its act won't work. First, Americans would have to stop watching. Look at the Southern Baptists. This rich, politically powerful organization of millions hasn't been able to bring off its boycott of Disney [for the benefits the company offers homosexual employees]. The urge to ride Space Mountain is even more powerful than homophobia.

> *"Violent and stupid entertainment is popular because it corresponds to reality, which is often violent and stupid."*

Real-Life Violence Is Pervasive in America

Violent and stupid entertainment is popular because it corresponds to reality, which is often violent and stupid. Take a society in which half the population is armed; with astronomical rates of rape, domestic violence, child abuse and murder; which fights one war after another and glories in it, has a bad case of jock worship, and Lord knows how many white people marinating in racial resentment like Benjamin Smith; in which the vast majority of parents hit their kids and think that's fine. Take a society in which people are told they should be able to have whatever they want, but only if they can pay for it and if they can't they're losers. Why wouldn't the inhabitants of such a society thrill to watch their psychosocial dramas enacted on screen?

It's always the same story: We meet the enemy and he is us.

Chapter 2

Does Violence in the Media Make Children and Teenagers More Violent?

CURRENT CONTROVERSIES

Chapter Preface

The April 20, 1999, murders at Columbine High School in Littleton, Colorado, and other similar school shootings, left the American public shocked and saddened. In the wake of the tragedy, parents, politicians, and researchers began searching for reasons why children and teenagers would resort to such violence. But as columnist John Leo explains, the political debate over youth violence soon broke down along party lines:

> Every time a disaster like the Colorado massacre occurs, Democrats want to focus on guns and Republicans want to talk about popular culture. . . . The Republicans can't say much about the gun lobby, because they accept too much of its money. The Democrats can't talk about Hollywood and the rest of the entertainment industry, because that's where so much of their funding comes from.

Following the Columbine tragedy, however, President Clinton hoped to move beyond these two traditional stances, and recognize that neither the availability of guns nor the level of violence in U.S. culture are the sole cause of youth violence. On May 10, 1999, Clinton held a White House summit meeting on youths and violence, promising that "we will not ask who takes the blame, but how we can all take responsibility."

At the summit, Clinton did take a somewhat critical stance toward the entertainment community. "We cannot pretend that there is no impact on our culture and our children that is adverse if there is too much violence coming out of what they see and experience," he said. The president also urged parents to "refuse to buy products which glorify violence."

Many observers faulted Clinton for not taking any substantial measures toward curbing either the availability of guns or the level of violence in the media. Former Republican presidential candidate Gary Bauer called the summit "a feel-good forum, lots of talk and not much action."

In the end, Clinton did make two contributions regarding media violence. The first was to call upon movie theater owners to check for IDs so that teenagers under age seventeen would not have access to R-rated movies. The second was to commission a year-long, $1 million study on whether the entertainment industry deliberately markets violent media products to children. Prior to the summit, the president also commissioned a new study by the surgeon general on how a variety of factors, including popular culture, mental illness, and guns, are involved in triggering violence in young people.

The new federal studies will surely help revive the debate over whether media violence contributes to real-life violence. The viewpoints in the following chapter offer insight into the research that has been done on this issue as they support or reject the claim that media violence causes children and teenagers to be more violent in their own lives.

Movie and Television Violence Makes Children Violent

by Gregg Easterbrook

About the author: *Gregg Easterbrook is a senior editor of the* New Republic.

Millions of teens have seen the 1996 movie *Scream,* a box-office and home-rental hit. Critics adored the film. The *Washington Post* declared that it "deftly mixes irony, self-reference, and social wry commentary." The *Los Angeles Times* hailed it as "a bravura, provocative send-up." *Scream* opens with a scene in which a teenage girl is forced to watch her jock boyfriend tortured and then disemboweled by two fellow students who, it will eventually be learned, want revenge on anyone from high school who crossed them. After jock boy's stomach is shown cut open and he dies screaming, the killers stab and torture the girl, then cut her throat and hang her body from a tree so that Mom can discover it when she drives up. A dozen students and teachers are graphically butchered in the film, while the characters make running jokes about murder. At one point, a boy tells a big-breasted friend she'd better be careful because the stacked girls always get it in horror films; in the next scene, she's grabbed, stabbed through the breasts, and murdered. Some provocative send-up, huh? The movie builds to a finale in which one of the killers announces that he and his accomplice started off by murdering strangers but then realized it was a lot more fun to kill their friends.

Murder as Sport

Now that two Colorado high schoolers have murdered twelve classmates and a teacher—often, it appears, first taunting their pleading victims, just like celebrity stars do in the movies!—some commentators have dismissed the role of violence in the images shown to the young, pointing out that horrific acts by children existed before celluloid or the phosphor screen. That is true—the

Leopold-Loeb murder of 1924, for example. But mass murders by the young, once phenomenally rare, are suddenly on the increase. Can it be coincidence that this increase is happening at the same time that Hollywood has begun to market the notion that mass murder is fun?

For, in cinema's never-ending quest to up the ante on violence, murder as sport is the latest frontier. Slasher flicks began this trend; most portray carnage from the killer's point of view, showing the victim cowering, begging, screaming as the blade goes in, treating each death as a moment of festivity for the killer. (Many killers seek feelings of power over their victims, criminology finds; by reveling in the pleas of victims, slasher movies promote this base emotion.) The 1994 movie *Natural Born Killers* depicted slaying the helpless not only as a way to have a grand time but also as a way to become a celebrity; several dozen onscreen murders are shown in that film, along with a discussion of how great it makes you feel to just pick people out at random and kill them. The 1994 movie *Pulp Fiction* presented hit men as glamour figures having loads of interesting fun; the actors were mainstream stars like John Travolta. The 1995 movie *Seven,* starring Brad Pitt, portrayed a sort of contest to murder in unusually grotesque ways. (Screenwriters now actually discuss, and critics comment on, which film's killings are most amusing.) The 1995 movie *The Basketball Diaries* contains an extended dream sequence in which the title character, played by teen heartthrob Leonardo DiCaprio, methodically guns down whimpering, pleading classmates at his high school. A rock soundtrack pulses, and the character smiles as he kills.

The new Hollywood tack of portraying random murder as a form of recreation does not come from schlock-houses. Disney's Miramax division, the same mainstream studio that produced *Shakespeare in Love,* is responsible for *Scream* and *Pulp Fiction.* Time-Warner is to blame for *Natural Born Killers* and actually ran television ads promoting this film as "delirious, daredevil fun." (After it was criticized for calling murder "fun," Time-Warner tried to justify *Killers* as social commentary; if you believe that, you believe *Godzilla* was really about biodiversity protection.) Praise and publicity for gratuitously violent movies come from the big media conglomerates, including the newspapers and networks that profit from advertising for films that glorify murder. Disney, now one of the leading promoters of violent images in American culture, even feels that what little kids need is more violence. Its Christmas 1998 children's movie *Mighty Joe Young* begins with an eight-year-old girl watching her mother being murdered. By the movie's end, it is 20 years later, and the killer has returned to stalk the grown daughter, pointing a gun in her face and announcing, "Now join your mother in hell." A Disney movie.

> *"The typical American boy or girl, studies find, will observe a stunning 40,000 dramatizations of killing by age 18."*

One reason Hollywood keeps reaching for ever-more-obscene levels of killing is that it must compete with television, which today routinely airs the kind of violence once considered shocking in theaters. According to studies conducted at Temple University, prime-time network (non-news) shows now average up to five violent acts per hour. In February, NBC ran in prime time the movie *Eraser,* not editing out an extremely graphic scene in which a killer pulls a gun on a bystander and blasts away. The latest TV movie based on *The Rockford Files,* which aired on CBS the night of the Colorado murders, opened with a scene of an eleven-year-old girl in short-shorts being stalked by a man in a black hood, grabbed, and dragged off, screaming. *The Rockford Files* is a comedy. Combining television and movies, the typical American boy or girl, studies find, will observe a stunning 40,000 dramatizations of killing by age 18.

A Causal Link Between Media Violence and Actual Violence

In the days after the Colorado slaughter, discussion of violent images in American culture was dominated by the canned positions of the anti-Hollywood right and the mammon-is-our-God film lobby. The debate missed three vital points: the distinction between what adults should be allowed to see (anything) and what the inchoate minds of children and adolescents should see; the way in which important liberal battles to win free expression in art and literature have been perverted into an excuse for antisocial video brutality produced by cynical capitalists; and the difference between censorship and voluntary acts of responsibility.

> *"The postwar murder rise in the United States began roughly a decade after TV viewing became common."*

The day after the Colorado shooting, Mike De Luca, an executive of New Line Cinema, maker of *The Basketball Diaries,* told *USA Today* that, when kids kill, "bad home life, bad parenting, having guns in the home" are "more of a factor than what we put out there for entertainment." Setting aside the disclosure that Hollywood now categorizes scenes of movie stars gunning down the innocent as "entertainment," De Luca is correct: studies do show that upbringing is more determinant of violent behavior than any other factor. But research also clearly shows that the viewing of violence can cause aggression and crime. So the question is, in a society already plagued by poor parenting and unlimited gun sales, why does the entertainment industry feel privileged to make violence even more prevalent?

Even when researchers factor out other influences such as parental attention, many peer-reviewed studies have found causal links between viewing phony violence and engaging in actual violence. A 1971 Surgeon General's report asserted a broad relationship between the two. Studies by Brandon Centerwall, an epidemiologist at the University of Wisconsin, have shown that the postwar murder rise in the United States began roughly a decade after TV viewing became common. Centerwall also found that, in South Africa, where television was not generally available until 1975, national murder rates started rising about a decade later. Violent computer games have not existed long enough to be the subject of many controlled studies, but experts expect it will be shown that playing such games in youth also correlates with destructive behavior. There's an eerie likelihood that violent movies and violent games amplify one another, the film and television images placing thoughts of carnage into the psyche while the games condition the trigger finger to act on those impulses.

> *"'Kids learn by observation. . . . If what they observe is violent, that's what they learn.'"*

Leonard Eron, a psychologist at the University of Michigan, has been tracking video violence and actual violence for almost four decades. His initial studies, in 1960, found that even the occasional violence depicted in 1950s television—to which every parent would gladly return today—caused increased aggression among eight-year-olds. By the adult years, Eron's studies find, those who watched the most TV and movies in childhood were much more likely to have been arrested for, or convicted of, violent felonies. Eron believes that ten percent of U.S. violent crime is caused by exposure to images of violence, meaning that 90 percent is not but that a ten percent national reduction in violence might be achieved merely by moderating the content of television and movies. "Kids learn by observation," Eron says. "If what they observe is violent, that's what they learn." To cite a minor but telling example, the introduction of vulgar language into American public discourse traces, Eron thinks, largely to the point at which stars like Clark Gable began to swear onscreen, and kids then imitated swearing as normative.

Children Are More Affected by Media Violence

Defenders of bloodshed in film, television, and writing often argue that depictions of killing don't incite real violence because no one is really affected by what they see or read; it's all just water off a duck's back. At heart, this is an argument against free expression. The whole reason to have a First Amendment is that people are influenced by what they see and hear: words and images do change minds, so there must be free competition among them. If what we say, write, or show has no consequences, why bother to have free speech?

Defenders of Hollywood bloodshed also employ the argument that, since millions of people watch screen mayhem and shrug, feigned violence has no causal relation to actual violence. After a horrific 1992 case in which a British gang acted out a scene from the slasher movie *Child's Play 3*, torturing a girl to death as the movie had shown, the novelist Martin Amis wrote dismissively in *The New Yorker* that he had rented *Child's Play 3* and watched the film, and it hadn't made him want to kill anyone, so what was the problem? But Amis isn't homicidal or unbalanced. For those on the psychological borderline, the calculus is different. There have, for example, been at least two instances of real-world shootings in which the guilty imitated scenes in *Natural Born Killers.*

Most telling, Amis wasn't affected by watching a slasher movie because Amis is not young. Except for the unbalanced, exposure to violence in video "is not so important for adults; adults can watch anything they want," Eron says. Younger minds are a different story. Children who don't yet understand the difference between illusion and reality may be highly affected by video violence. Between the ages of two and eight, hours of viewing violent TV programs and movies correlates closely to felonies later in life; the child comes to see hitting, stabbing, and shooting as normative acts. The link between watching violence and engaging in violence continues up to about the age of 19, Eron finds, after which most people's characters have been formed, and video mayhem no longer correlates to destructive behavior.

Blaming Guns—While Also Glamorizing Them

Trends in gun availability do not appear to explain the murder rise that has coincided with television and violent films. Research by John Lott Jr., of the University of Chicago Law School, shows that the percentage of homes with guns has changed little throughout the postwar era. What appears to have changed is the willingness of people to fire their guns at one another. Are adolescents now willing to use guns because violent images make killing seem acceptable or even cool? Following the Colorado slaughter, the *New York Times* ran a recounting of other postwar mass murders staged by the young, such as the 1966 [Austin] Texas tower killings, and noted that they all happened before the advent of the Internet or shock rock, which seemed to the *Times* to absolve the modern media. But all the mass killings by the young occurred after 1950—after it became common to watch violence on television.

When horrific murders occur, the film and television industries routinely attempt to transfer criticism to the weapons used. Just after the Colorado shootings, for instance, TV talk-show host Rosie O'Donnell called for a constitutional amendment banning all firearms. How strange that O'Donnell didn't call instead for a boycott of Sony or its production company, Columbia Tristar—a film studio from which she has received generous paychecks and whose current offerings include *8MM*, which glamorizes the sexual murder of young women, and *The Replacement Killers,* whose hero is a hit man and which depicts dozens of gun murders. Handguns should be licensed, but that hardly excuses the convenient sanctimony of blaming the crime on the weapon, rather than on what resides in the human mind.

> *"Children who don't yet understand the difference between illusion and reality may be highly affected by video violence."*

56

And, when it comes to promoting adoration of guns, Hollywood might as well be the National Rifle Association's marketing arm. An ever-increasing share of film and television depicts the firearm as something the virile must have and use, if not an outright sexual aid. Check the theater section of any newspaper, and you will find an ever-higher percentage of movie ads in which the stars are prominently holding guns. Keanu Reeves, Uma Thurman, Laurence Fishburne, Geena Davis, Woody Harrelson, and Mark Wahlberg are just a few of the hip stars who have posed with guns for movie advertising. Hollywood endlessly congratulates itself for reducing the depiction of cigarettes in movies and movie ads. Cigarettes had to go, the film industry admitted, because glamorizing them gives the wrong idea to kids. But the glamorization of firearms, which is far more dangerous, continues. Today, even female stars who otherwise consider themselves politically aware will model in sexualized poses with guns. Ads for the new movie *Goodbye Lover* show star Patricia Arquette nearly nude, with very little between her and the viewer but her handgun.

> **"When it comes to promoting adoration of guns, Hollywood might as well be the National Rifle Association's marketing arm."**

The Profitability of Violent Cinema

But doesn't video violence merely depict a stark reality against which the young need to be warned? American society is far too violent, yet the forms of brutality highlighted in the movies and on television—prominently "thrill" killings and serial murders—are pure distortion. Nearly 99 percent of real murders result from robberies, drug deals, and domestic disputes; figures from research affiliated with the FBI's behavioral sciences division show an average of only about 30 serial or "thrill" murders nationally per year. Thirty is plenty horrifying enough, but, at this point, each of the major networks and movie studios alone depicts more "thrill" and serial murders annually than that. By endlessly exploiting the notion of the "thrill" murder, Hollywood and television present to the young an entirely imaginary image of a society in which killing for pleasure is a common event. The publishing industry . . . also distorts for profit the frequency of "thrill" murders.

The profitability of violent cinema is broadly dependent on the "down-rating" of films—movies containing extreme violence being rated only R instead of NC-17 (the new name for X)—and the lax enforcement of age restrictions regarding movies. Teens are the best market segment for Hollywood; when moviemakers claim their violent movies are not meant to appeal to teens, they are simply lying. The millionaire status of actors, directors, and studio heads—and the returns of the mutual funds that invest in movie companies—depends on not restricting teen access to theaters or film rentals. Studios in effect control the movie ratings board and endlessly lobby it not to label extreme violence with an NC-17, the only form of rating that is actually enforced. *Natural Born Killers,* for example, received an R following Time-Warner lobbying, despite its repeated close-up murders and one charming scene in which the stars kidnap a high school girl and argue about whether it would be more fun to kill her before or after raping her. Since its inception, the movie ratings board has put its most restrictive rating on any realistic representation of lovemaking, while sanctioning ever-more-graphic depictions of murder and torture. In economic terms, the board's pro-violence bias gives studios an incentive to present more death and mayhem, confident that ratings officials will smile with approval.

When R-and-X battles were first fought, intellectual sentiment regarded the ratings system as a way of blocking the young from seeing films with political content, such as *Easy Rider,* or discouraging depictions of sexuality; ratings were perceived as the rubes' counterattack against cinematic sophistication. But, in the 1960s, murder after murder after murder was not standard cinema fare. The most controversial violent film of that era, *A Clockwork Orange,* depicted a total of one killing, which was heard but not on-camera. (*Clockwork Orange* also had genuine political content, unlike most of today's big-studio movies.) In an era of runaway screen violence, the '60s ideal that the young should be allowed to see what they want has been corrupted. In this, trends in video mirror the misuse of liberal ideals generally.

Anti-censorship battles of this century were fought on firm ground, advocating the right of films to tackle social and sexual issues (the 1930s Hays office forbid among other things cinematic mention of cohabitation) and free access to works of literature such as *Ulysses, Story of O,* and the original version of Norman Mailer's *The Naked and the Dead.* Struggles against censors established that suppression of film or writing is wrong.

> *"Hollywood and television present to the young an entirely imaginary image of a society in which killing for pleasure is a common event."*

But to say that nothing should be censored is very different from saying that everything should be shown. Today, Hollywood and television have twisted the First Amendment concept that occasional repulsive or worthless expression must be protected, so as to guarantee freedom for works of genuine political content or artistic merit, into a new standard in which constitutional freedoms are employed mainly to safeguard works that make no pretense of merit. In the new standard, the bulk of what's being protected is repulsive or worthless, with the meritorious work the rare exception.

Not only is there profit for the performers, producers, management, and shareholders of firms that glorify violence, so, too, is there profit for politicians. Many conservative or Republican politicians who denounce Hollywood eagerly accept its lucre. Bob Dole's 1995 anti-Hollywood speech was not followed up by any anti-Hollywood legislation or campaign-funds strategy. After the Colorado murders, President Clinton declared, "Parents should take this moment to ask what else they can do to shield children from violent images and experiences that warp young perceptions." But Clinton was careful to avoid criticizing Hollywood, one of the top sources of public backing and campaign contributions for him and his would-be successor, Vice President Al Gore. The president had nothing specific to propose on film violence—only that parents should try to figure out what to do.

A Call for Restraint

When television producers say it is the parents' obligation to keep children away from the tube, they reach the self-satire point of warning that their own product is unsuitable for consumption. The situation will improve somewhat beginning in 2000, by which time all new TVs must be sold with the "V chip"—supported by Clinton and Gore—which will allow parents to block violent shows. But it will be at least a decade before the majority of the nation's sets include the chip, and who knows how adept young minds will prove at defeating it? Rather than relying on a technical fix that will take many years to achieve an effect, TV producers could simply stop churning out the gratuitous violence. Television could dramatically reduce its output of scenes of killing and still depict violence in news broadcasts, documentaries, and the occasional show in which the horrible is genuinely relevant. Reduction in violence is not censorship; it is placing social responsibility before profit.

The movie industry could practice the same kind of restraint without sacrificing profitability. In this regard, the big Hollywood studios, including Disney, look craven and exploitative compared to, of all things, the porn-video industry. Repulsive material occurs in underground porn, but, in the products sold by the mainstream triple-X distributors such as Vivid Video (the MGM of the erotica business), violence is never, ever, ever depicted—because that would be irresponsible. Women and men perform every conceivable explicit

> *"Hollywood and television do need to hear the words 'shame, shame.'"*

act in today's mainstream porn, but what is shown is always consensual and almost sunnily friendly. Scenes of rape or sexual menace never occur, and scenes of sexual murder are an absolute taboo.

It is beyond irony that today Sony and Time-Warner eagerly market explicit depictions of women being raped, sexually assaulted, and sexually murdered, while the mainstream porn industry would never dream of doing so. But, if money is all that matters, the point here is that mainstream porn is violence-free and yet risqué and highly profitable. Surely this shows that Hollywood could voluntarily step back from the abyss of glorifying violence and still retain its edge and its income.

Following the Colorado massacre, Republican presidential candidate Gary Bauer declared to a campaign audience, "In the America I want, all of these producers and directors, they would not be able to show their faces in public" because fingers "would be pointing at them and saying, 'Shame, shame.'" The statement sent chills through anyone fearing right-wing thought-control. But Bauer's final clause is correct—Hollywood and television do need to hear the words "shame, shame." The cause of the shame should be removed voluntarily, not to stave off censorship, but because it is the responsible thing to do.

Put it this way. The day after a teenager guns down the sons and daughters of studio executives in a high school in Bel Air or Westwood, Disney and Time-Warner will stop glamorizing murder. Do we have to wait until that day?

Popular Music Contributes to Teenage Violence

by Thomas L. Jipping

About the author: *Thomas L. Jipping is director of the Free Congress Foundation's Center for Law and Democracy, a conservative think tank in Washington, D.C.*

On April 20, 1999, two teenagers killed 12 of their peers, a teacher, and themselves at Columbine High School in Littleton, Colorado. A few days later, Colorado Governor Bill Owens warned in a radio address of a "virus loose within our culture.". . . Some popular music is part of this cultural virus, which can help lead some young people to violence.

Five days after the massacre, Tim Russert, host of NBC's *Meet the Press*, reported on the show that the Littleton killers idolized shock-rocker Marilyn Manson, described even by the music press as an "ultra-violent satanic rock monstrosity." Other teenage killers have done the same. These include Kip Kinkel, who murdered his parents and two students at Thurston High School in Springfield, Oregon; Andrew Wurst, who killed a teacher at an eighth-grade dance in Edinboro, Pennsylvania; and Luke Woodham, who murdered his parents and a classmate in Pearl, Mississippi.

The pattern was the same as other violent youths whose plans were foiled. A Leesburg, Virginia, teenager suspended for threatening students who made fun of his literary work was fascinated with Marilyn Manson. Five Wisconsin teenagers who had carefully planned a bloodbath at their school in revenge for being teased were Manson fans.

Marilyn Manson and the Littleton Massacre

Dismissing all this as coincidence becomes increasingly difficult. The facts of these and other instances of youth violence parallel not just the generally violent themes but the specifically violent action in the music these boys consumed. Manson repeatedly dwells on revenge and violence against the objects of his hatred. In "Lunchbox," he says that the next bully who "fu**s with me" is "gonna get my metal. . . . Pow pow pow." In "Irresponsible Hate Anthem," he responds to the "selective judgments" of others by saying "get your gun." In "The Beautiful People," he says there is "no time to discriminate, hate every motherfu**er that's in your way." In "Man That You Fear," he warns that "I'll make everyone pay and you will see . . . the boy that you loved is the monster you fear." And in "The Suck for Your Solution," he says that "I'm gonna hate you tomorrow because you make me hate you today."

Ordained in the Church of Satan, Manson wrote in the foreword to the book *Satan Speaks* that its late founder, Anton LaVey, "was the most righteous man I've ever known." On CNN's *The American Edge* program, Manson explained his view that "you are your own god. It's a lot about self-preservation. . . . It's the part of you that no longer has hope in mankind. And you realize that you are the only thing you believe in." In one interview, Manson explained that when he attended a public school "they would always kick my ass. . . . So I didn't end up having a lot of friends and music was the only thing I had to enjoy. So I got into [heavy metal rock bands] Kiss, Black Sabbath and things like that."

Despite all these parallels, Manson's response to the Littleton massacre was predictable: "The media has unfairly scapegoated the music industry . . . and has speculated—with no basis in truth—that artists like myself are in some way to blame." He is wrong. There is a sound basis for concluding that some popular music can help lead some young people to violence. That conclusion rests on three pillars.

Research Has Proved the Link Between Media Violence and Actual Violence

First, as the American Medical Association (AMA) concluded in September 1996, the "link between media violence and real life violence has been proven by science time and again." Many leading medical associations, as well as commissions and task forces created to study the issue, have over the last three decades documented that, in the words of columnist William Raspberry, "television violence begets real-world violence."

Professor Leonard Eron concluded in a speech at the Harvard University School of Public Health that literally hundreds of studies provide "convincing evidence that the observation of violence, as seen in standard everyday television entertainment, does affect the aggressive behavior of the viewer." One writer reported that

> *"There is a sound basis for concluding that some popular music can help lead some young people to violence."*

"more than 1,000 studies since 1955 have linked media violence and aggressive behavior." A television network's own study concluded that more than one-fourth of young violent offenders had consciously imitated crime techniques learned from television.

The American people share the same conclusion. In fact, polls reveal that the percentage of Americans concerned that media violence contributes to real-life violence has grown by 50 percent during the 1990s.

The most common response by the television industry is that programming merely reflects what people already wish to consume, that the medium is entirely reactive and does not itself cause anything. In addition to common sense and experience, research evidence exists that this may not be true. A group of European and American researchers, for example, found that "the data across nations support the conclusion that viewing televised violence leads to aggressive behaviour and not vice versa."

Second, music is as powerful as television in its impact on people in general.

In September 1985, Joseph Steussay, professor of music history at the University of Texas, testified in U.S. Senate hearings that "tons of research has been done on the interrelationship of music and human behavior. . . . [M]usic affects human behavior. It affects our moods, our attitudes, our emotions, and our behavior." Pharmacologist Dr. Arram Goldstein of Stanford University found that 96 percent of people got their biggest thrills from music. Researcher Anne Rosenfeld put it well, describing the power of music as "a miracle akin to that of language. . . . But music is more than a language."

Third, music is more powerful than television for young people in particular. The AMA concluded in a 1989 report that music has a greater influ-

> *"'[M]usic affects . . . our moods, our attitudes, our emotions, and our behavior.'"*

ence than television on the lives of teenagers. Two other researchers more recently confirmed that "the average teenager listens to 10,500 hours of rock music during the years between the 7th and 12th grades, and music surpasses television as an influence in teenagers' lives." Polls show that teens consider musicians as heroes far more than even athletes and rate music ahead of religion and books as factors that greatly influence their generation.

Music Affects Listeners' Attitudes and Behavior

The music industry, like the television industry, claims it merely reflects and does not influence. In a commentary written for *Billboard* magazine, Hilary Rosen, president of the Recording Industry Association of America, argues that "lyrics, in essence, exhibit the action—they don't cause it. . . . [M]usic cannot cause action." This position is as false as it is self-serving. Sheila Davis, adjunct professor of lyric writing at New York University, makes the point that songs "are more than mere mirrors of society; they are a potent force in the shaping of it. . . . [P]opular songs provide the primary 'equipment for living' for America's youth."

Three categories of research dispute Rosen's disclaimer. First, research establishes that music affects basic attitudes and values. The author of a major book on satanism writes that "Dr. T.L. Tashjian, chair of the department of psychiatry at Mount Sinai Hospital in Philadelphia, has found significant effects of rock music on the formation of values and worldview among children."

Second, music affects behavior. Studies have found, for example, that consumers of music with harmful themes are more approving of antisocial behaviors and attitudes and that consumption "correlates with increasing discomfort in family situations, a preference for friends over family, and poor academic performance."

> *"Consumers of music with harmful themes are more approving of antisocial behaviors and attitudes."*

Third, and perhaps most disturbing, consumers of negative or destructive messages listen and internalize those messages more than consumers of more neutral messages. One study found that "fans of rock music containing potentially negative themes (i.e., suicide, homicide, and satanic themes) were more likely to report that they knew all of the words to their favorite songs and that the lyrics were important to their experience of the music." Professor Hannelore Wass and her colleagues similarly found that fans of heavy metal music listen more, know the words better, and actually agree with the words more than fans of general rock music. She concluded that her findings "seem to dispel the notion advanced by the recording industry that teenagers are only interested in the sound of music, don't know the lyrics, and listen strictly for fun."

Public opinion parallels the evidence about music, as it does the evidence about television. Two different 1995 surveys found that more teenagers than adults believe popular music encourages antisocial behavior. A *Newsweek* analysis said popular music lyrics contribute to the "culture of aggression."

Destructive Themes

Understanding the power of music, particularly in the lives of young people, is the first step. Reviewing the messages or themes delivered by this powerful medium completes the picture. Two conclusions are inescapable regarding rock and rap music, the most popular genres of music among young people today. First, negative or destructive themes are now the rule rather than the exception. Second, some popular music actively promotes these messages.

The American Academy of Pediatrics has concluded that "rock music has undergone dramatic changes since its introduction 30 years ago and is an issue of vital interest and concern for parents and pediatricians." While 25 percent of the top-selling recordings in 1990 were hard rock or heavy metal releases, by 1995 only 10 of the 40 most popular CDs were free of profanity or lyrics dealing with drugs, violence, and sex. As Dr. Paul King, clinical assistant professor of child and adolescent psychiatry at the University of Tennessee, describes it: "The message of heavy metal is that there is a higher power in control of the world and that power is violence—often violence presided over by Satan."

Similarly, a definitive history of rap music says that "the so-called gangsta

genre of rap" is now "the leading music genre in hip ho
Pitts describes this rap style and "the sound of unredee
lieved ugliness." One reviewer has called N.W.A. founc
platinum 1991 album *Death Certificate* an "exercise in i
by the Geto Boys includes a song titled "Mind of a Lu
ments of necrophilia, murder, and other violent acts."

Heavy metal rock music and gangsta rap not only inc
mote negative or destructive themes. A popular women'i
that "in addition to the typical teen themes of fast cars, |
change, many heavy metal groups dwell on topics suc
abuse, violence and rape." *Time* magazine says: "Rock
dominant—and potentially destructive—part of teenage c
covers and music videos, particularly in the rock genre ca
manticize bondage, sexual assaults and murder."

Professor Carl Raschke writes: "Heavy metal does not n
much as it artistically stylizes, aggrandizes, beautifies, we
chantment around what would otherwise be lesser and ordii
ior. . . . Heavy metal is a true aesthetics of violence. It is a m
tactic of consecrating violent terror, of divinizing it."

Gangsta rap promotes violence in the same way. One edi
this way:

> The most effective rejoinder comes from Mike Davis's *City of*
> tory of Los Angeles, where gangster rap was born. "In suppos
> bare the reality of the streets, 'telling it like it is,'" Mr. Davis wri
> offer an uncritical mirror to fantasy power trips of violence
> greed." Rappers, take note: The key phrase is "uncritical mirror
> "plays" at rape and murder in a way that celebrates them.

The pattern here is obvious. Heavy metal and gangsta rap "
manticize," "stylize," "aggrandize," "beautify," "consecrate," an
critical mirror" for violence. The American Academy of Pediat
that, in so doing, this music contributes to "new morbidities"—
pression, suicide, and homicide—in young people. These phy
were doing something more than, in Marilyn Manson's words, "u
goat[ing] the music industry." Similarly, the AMA warned that "th
tion of drug and alcohol use, suicide, violence, demonology, sex
tion, racism and bigotry [in some rock music] could be harmful to
people." The most prestigious medical society in America was afte
more important than, in Rosen's words, "blaming music for society'

Parents Can Take Action

A wise sage once said that everything has a frame of reference. If
sion about popular music is framed in terms of taste, it is pointles
dence shows persuasively, however, that the discussion should be

of harm. This more serious perspective suggests several action steps.

st, parents must visit the record stores in their area and do three things—
se, browse, and browse. This will reveal what is for sale and that some
dings already have labels warning of explicit lyrics.

cond, parents should visit those stores again and do three things—inquire,
ire, inquire. Does the store prohibit sales of labeled recordings to minors?
Labeled recordings are the audio version of *Hustler* magazine, and it makes no sense to restrict one but not the other. Parents should pressure the management to adopt such a policy, including by threatening to take their business elsewhere.

> *Heavy metal rock music and 'angsta rap not only include ut actually promote negative or destructive themes."*

hird, concerned citizens should use their power as stockholders and con-
ners to pressure manufacturers to stop producing harmful cultural products.
is is where the difference between taste and harm is critical.

ourth, concerned citizens should aggressively exercise their freedom of
eech and denounce harmful cultural products such as the music discussed
re. Sound arguments supported with the facts could, for example, become
blicized resolutions adopted by city councils, service organizations, and PTA
apters. Physicians, clinical social workers, and others with experience work-
g directly with young people could add their voices as well.

Finally, policymakers should consider applying to recordings the same restric-
ons that apply to visual pornography and indecent television or radio program-
ing. The medium transmitting the cultural damage is irrelevant; indeed, the ev-
dence shows that music is more powerful than other media. Public policy must,
f course, meet fundamental constitutional requirements. If this is an issue of
arm, however, pursuing this goal in a responsible manner might be appropriate.

Marilyn Manson is simply wrong that there is "no basis in truth" for the spec-
lation that he and similar artists contribute to youth violence. In 1956, the *New
York Times* called rock music "a communicable disease." Today, some popular
music remains part of the cultural virus that can lead some young people to violence. The debate is not about taste but about harm. As one writer put it:

> People consume rage as entertainment; they plunk their money down, turn up
> the volume, and shout themselves hoarse. They shout Public Enemy's black
> nationalism, Slayer's ambivalent Satanism, Living Colour's warnings of envi-
> ronmental disaster, Nine Inch Nails' self-laceration, Anthrax's moral dialec-
> tics, Skid Row's triumphal Machismo. For a little while, it feels like actual
> power—until—the music stops.

Or until the killing starts.

Violent Video Games Teach Children to Enjoy Killing

by Dave Grossman

About the author: *Dave Grossman is a retired army officer and the author of* On Killing: The Psychological Cost of Learning to Kill in War and Society *and the co-author of* Stop Teaching Our Kids to Kill: A Call to Action Against TV, Movie, and Video Game Violence.

Editor's note: The following viewpoint was given in May 1999 as testimony before the House of Representatives Judiciary Committee on Youth Culture and Violence.

My background is as a West Point psychology professor and Army Ranger, [and as] a professor of military science. I have written three encyclopedia entries on the process of military enabling of killing, and the entry in the *Oxford Companion to American Military History,* . . . and the book, *On Killing,* that is being used as a text in peace studies programs around the world and in places like West Point and law enforcement academies.

From that perspective, I want you to understand what the military knows about killing. There is a broad leap, a vast chasm, between being a healthy American citizen and being able to snuff another human being's life out. There has to be a bridge, there has to be a gap. In World War II, we taught our soldiers to fire at bull's eye targets. They fought well. They fought bravely. But we realized there was a flaw in our training when they came on the battlefield and they saw no bull's eyes. And they were not able to transition from training to reality.

Murder Simulators

Since World War II, we have introduced a wide variety of simulators. The first of those simulators were pop-up human targets. When those targets appeared in front of the soldier, they learned to fire, and fire instinctively. When real human beings popped up in front of them, they could transfer the data from that simulator.

Testimony given by Dave Grossman before the House of Representatives Judiciary Committee on Youth Culture and Violence, May 13, 1999.

Today, we use more advanced simulators. The law enforcement community uses a simulator that is a large screen television with human beings on it, firing a gun that is identical to what you will see in any video arcade, except in the arcade the safety catch is turned off. The army has a device. . . . The last time I trained on this device, it had a label on it that said "Nintendo." I have confirmed with the Arkansas National Guard where I trained that this device has a Nintendo stamp on it.

The army uses this device, a plastic M-16, that you fire at a screen, because it is an extraordinary device to train marksmanship skills. Now, in any video arcade in America, we have got children playing identical devices. The industry has to ask how they can market one device to the military, whoever is marketing it, and then turn around and give the same device

> *"We have mass murder simulators that can truly teach you how to commit a mass murder even before you put your hands on a gun."*

to your children, and claim that it is harmless. The video game "Doom" is being marketed and has been licensed to the United States Marine Corps. The Marine Corps is using it as an excellent tactical training device. How can the same device be provided indiscriminately to children over the Internet, and yet the Marine Corps continue to use this device?

We all know about the power of flight simulators. We have flight simulators that can teach you to fly without ever touching an airplane, driving simulators that teach you how to drive, and we have mass murder simulators that can truly teach you how to commit a mass murder even before you put your hands on a gun.

Now, in these mass murders we have seen, usually the child is out to kill their girlfriend. Very often, the first victim . . . has been a girlfriend. But they keep going. And the law enforcement officers ask, "why did you keep going?" And one of the answers that one child provided a few years back was, "well, it just seemed like I had momentum." Well, those of us that study simulators understand that you get in a routine, just like a child in a fire drill, like a pilot in a flight simulator, a set of automatic conditioned responses has set in. You hold a weapon in your hands and you mow down every living creature in front of you until you run out of ammo or you run out of targets. That is what they have been conditioned and programmed to do, as we program soldiers, but without the safeguards.

The Problem Is Worsening

Now, what we have before us is a new national video game. The children are invested in racking up the new high score in a national video game. The high scores on this game, instead of getting the three-letter initials in the arcade, gets their picture on *Time* magazine and on every television in America. I have been predicting for close to a year now that the next major school shooting will include bombs. How could we have known that? Well, because if you want to get up to the upper levels in a video game and get that high body count, you have got to have instruments of mass destruction. And every video game incorporates that at the higher levels, we are scripting the children and they are carrying out the scripts. As I travel around the country as one of the nation's premier law enforcement trainers, training the Federal officers, training the Texas Rangers, a battalion of Green Berets, the Australian Federal Police, the Canadian Mounties, as I train these individuals, universally, across America, I am told there are more attempted school shootings this year than last year. We are just better at nipping them in the bud. And we have ever more police officers, ever more metal detectors, children that courageously report the presence of the guns, but we are keeping the lid on a pressure cooker. The willingness of the children to commit these crimes has gone up and up and up.

Many people say it is the parents' responsibility to deal with this matter. Well, it is, without a doubt. But it is the parents' responsibility to protect the child from guns, explosives, drugs, alcohol, tobacco, and pornography. And on all of those substances, society helps the parents. Society regulates guns, explosives, drugs, alcohol, tobacco, and pornography. And we say that anybody that provides that substance to a child is a criminal. In the same way, the time may have come for us to say that anybody who provides these toxic substances to children is a criminal. Since 1957, in America, the per capita assault rate has gone up sevenfold. In Canada, since 1964, the per capita assault rate

> *"There is a clear link between media violence and violent behavior in children."*

has gone up approximately fivefold. In the last 15 years, in European nations, the per capita assault rate has gone up approximately fivefold in Norway and Greece, fourfold in Australia and New Zealand. It has tripled in Sweden, and doubled in seven other European nations.

Now, the only common denominator in all of those nations is that we are feeding our children death and horror and destruction as entertainment. And the worst of these is the violent video games, the simulated training devices.

The Research Is Clear

Now, in 1972, the Surgeon General released a report about the link between media violence and real-world violence. I was on *Meet the Press* last week with the Surgeon General. He said, "Sure, I can do a new study, but why don't we go back to 1972 and look at the 1972 study, and start taking action."

Why don't we go back to 1972 and take a look at the 1972 study? The Surgeon General was very straightforward about it. We do not need more research. We have over 4,000 sound, scholarly studies.

In 1982, the National Institute of Mental Health assessed over 2,500 scholarly studies and came to the conclusion that there is a clear link between media violence and violent behavior in children. In 1992, the American Psychiatric Association report said, quote: "The scientific debate is over." The APA has made definitive statements. Now, we see media representatives standing up and defending their industry. And I submit that that is the equivalent of an agriculture professor, with all of his background, trying to refute the American Medical Association on tobacco and cancer.

The real media critic is not Siskel and Ebert. It is the American Medical Association. And it is time to put them in charge of the Federal Communications Commission and other organizations, and listen to what they have to say—the American Academy of Pediatrics and others.

Now, 16 million kids supposedly have access to guns. By my calculations, 6/10,000ths of a percent of the kids with access to guns will abuse that right. But because of 6/10,000ths of a percent, we as a society agree that anybody that puts a gun in the hands of a child is a criminal. Well, in this way, these murder simulators are also dangerous instruments that need to be restrained from the hands of children. They teach children the motor skills to kill, like military training devices do. And then they turn around and teach them to like it—like the military would never do. Not everybody who smokes cigarettes gets cancer, but everybody is sickened by it. Not everybody who ingests media violence is a killer, but they are all sickened by it.

Dr. George Gerbner's research indicates what is called the Mean World Syndrome. They are more likely to be abusive to their own children in the years to come. They are more likely to be fearful. The adrenaline/hormonal responses go up in these individuals. They are all profoundly influenced, and our society is subsequently influenced by them.

A Gun Control Issue, Not a Free Speech Issue

The American Civil Liberties Union (ACLU) has not made a clear comment on these video games, these killing simulators. One representative told me, "I cannot remotely see the ACLU defending the right of 5-year-olds or 9-year-olds at the local arcade to practice killing human beings."

You see, this is not a First Amendment issue. These are firearms trainers. And this is a Second Amendment issue. The National Rifle Association's Wayne LaPierre even said this "sounds like a Second Amendment issue to me." And as such, these things should be regulated, just like guns. Anybody who gives a child a gun is a criminal. Anybody who gives unrestricted access to these devices are criminals.

Take the Michael Carneal case, in Paducah, Kentucky. A 14-year-old boy who had never fired a gun before in his life takes a .22 caliber pistol to school and fires eight shots. The FBI says the average law enforcement officer, in a real-world engagement, hits with less than one bullet in five. Michael Carneal fired eight shots. He got eight hits on eight different children; five of them head shots, the other three upper torso. Where did he get that from? From the video games. He had played those video games over and over again and had become a master killer. The heads of every major national and international law enforcement training organization has personally told me that they are willing to testify in the Paducah case for free, to talk about the link between these video simulators as they are used by the law enforcement community and their impact on children.

> *"[Violent video games] teach children the motor skills to kill. . . . And then they turn around and teach them to like it."*

In 1997, the overall violent crime rate went down 2 percent, but law enforcement fatalities went up 21 percent. The individuals that law enforcement agents face are ever-more trained, ever-better qualified, and they are concerned that children have their own private police-quality firearms training sitting in the arcade and they are able to play it.

Now, the research on this data is comprehensive. Look at the research on simulators. Look at the billions of dollars spent on flight simulators and why. Then look at the research on violent media. And then combine that research together and understand how powerful it is.

Education, Legislation, and Litigation

Some people say we need new research on these. We have already done billions of dollars of research, and we can combine those ingredients. We are calling for three things. Education, legislation, and litigation. We must educate America's parents, as a comprehensive national program, about what the AMA and the APA and the Surgeon General says about the link between violent media and violence in their children.

Legislation: these devices that you see the ads for out there, these devices are law enforcement training devices that need to be legislated. And they are not even remotely a first.

And, finally, litigation: Three ads here from the video game industry. One is for a joy-stick in a children's magazine. When you pull the trigger, it bucks in your hand like a gun. The ad says: "Psychologists say it is important to feel something when you kill."

Another ad is, again, in a children's magazine, for a game that says: "Kill your friends guilt-free." Here is another ad, again, in a children's magazine, for a video game. It says: "More fun than shooting the neighbor's cat."

Now, the Supreme Court has determined that a book called *The Assassin's Handbook* was not protected by the First Amendment because it openly advocated murder and killing and taught the skills. If a book, if a set of texts is not protected by the First Amendment, then are these firearms simulators protected?

We need to begin holding the producers and profiteers of these video games accountable for the toxic substance they are pouring into our children's lives.

Violent Movies Do Not Make Children Violent

by Jack Valenti

About the author: *Jack Valenti is president and chief executive officer of the Motion Picture Association of America.*

Editor's note: The following viewpoint is excerpted from Valenti's May 1999 testimony before the Senate Committee on Commerce, Science, and Transportation, at a hearing entitled Marketing Violence to Children.

What happened at Columbine High School in Colorado was a senseless act of mindless malice. Every sane American recoils in horror. There is rage in the land. There are outcries to ban, abolish, and quarantine by legislative fiat what many believe to be source beds of fatal mischief. . . .

Accusatory Fingers Point Toward Movies

Let's discuss movies. Accusatory fingers point toward films as a prime villain. [In 1998] the entire movie industry produced over 550 films. When that many movies are made, some of them are bound to be slovenly conceived. In a free society, no one can command 'only good movies be produced.' Which is why I will not defend all movies. Some few in my judgment cross a smudged, ill-illuminated line where the acceptable becomes unsuitable, and I'll have no part of them. The great majority of films, some of them rising to the highest point to which the creative spirit can soar, don't warrant being lumped with a number of movies whose worth is questionable. Edmund Burke was right when he said, "You cannot indict an entire society." Neither should anyone condemn the many because of the porous quality of the very few. Moreover, American parents have the supreme right not to patronize what they judge to be soiling to their children's future. The parental bill of rights declares the power of parents to turn away from that which they don't want their family to listen to or watch. Banish them from your home, refuse to patronize them outside [it].

Testimony given by Jack Valenti before the Senate Committee on Commerce, Science, and Transportation, May 4, 1999.

The Movie/TV Industry Has an Obligation to Be Responsible

I do earnestly believe that the movie/TV industry has a solemn obligation. Each creative team must examine their work from a personal perspective. Is there gratuitous violence, language or sensuality? If there is, then the creative team, on its own, without any nagging or commands from anyone else, ought to exile whatever is gratuitous without dismaying the dramatic narrative that is the core of the story. I wholeheartedly endorse that kind of creative scrutiny.

Years ago many of us in the movie world came to the conclusion that we had a duty to inform parents about film content. This is the prime reason why for over thirty years a voluntary movie rating system, created and implemented by film producers and theater owners, has been in place. These ratings give advance cautionary warnings to parents so they can decide what movies they want their children to see or not to see. Only parents are capable of making such decisions. Some 75% of parents with children under thirteen find this rating system Very Useful to Fairly Useful in helping them guide their children's movie viewing.

A comparable rating system is operative in television, offering information to parents about TV shows. Soon, there will be available in large supply the so-called V-Chip whose aim it is to give parents more power over the TV viewing of their children.

> *"If the media was at fault . . . everyone of the . . . 1,850 students at Columbine would all be killers because . . . the students all watch the same movies."*

Parents have to tend to their children's TV viewing, seriously, tenaciously, else they cannot indict others for their lack of monitoring TV watching in the home. For example, too many parents are agreeing to give their young children their own TV set, in their own room, thereby losing control over what their children are watching. But that is a parental decision they alone can make.

The movie industry has played, and is playing, an important role in our society, and will continue to do so. American movies travel the world, where they are hospitably received and enthusiastically patronized. Our movies, from *Mr. Smith Goes to Washington* to *Saving Private Ryan,* from *Ben Hur* to *Star Wars,* captivate audiences everywhere. Entertainment created in America is one of this nation's proudest artistic and commercial assets. We produce for this country huge amounts of surplus balance of trade at a time when the country bleeds from trade deficits. (It is ironic that Japan, which devours American films and TV programs, has one of the lowest crime rates in the world!)

Listen to the Children

We (meaning parents and citizens, Congress, White House, professionals in the field of education, science and business) should listen to the children, the youngsters in grammar school, middle school and high school. They are best equipped to tell us if the media is the complete villain, if what they hear and see infects them, and soils their best intentions. They know better than their elders about peer pressure and rejection and cliques and the mean alternatives that tantalize and entice them. Are we truly listening to them?

On Thursday, April 29, 1999, Jeff Greenfield (CNN) had a 'conversation' with students. Two of those students were from Columbine High School. One of them, a lovely senior named Alisha Basore, was queried about the impact of the media on unnatural behavior. She responded that the media was a minor force in distorting students' values. If the media was at fault, she said, everyone of the some 1,850 students at Columbine would all be killers because, as she pointed out, the students all watch the same movies and TV programs, listen to the same music, play the same video games. By her side was the other Columbine student, Josh Nielsen, who confirmed Alisha's remarks and said it wasn't the media, but rather that the two killers were crazy.

Let's listen to the children.

Popular Music Does Not Make Teenagers Violent

by David E. Nantais

About the author: *David E. Nantais is studying philosophy and theology at Loyola University in Chicago.*

Billy Joel once said in an interview on "60 Minutes" that he thinks of his songs as his children. He remarked that some of them go on to become doctors and lawyers (presumably the Top 40 Hits), while others grow up to be bums. I wonder if Billy believes that any of his "kids" could ever grow up to be mass murderers or terrorists.

An Easy Scapegoat

Ever since the horrible shootings in Littleton, Colorado, many groups around the country have been engaged in quasi-psychological ranting about the negative effects pop music has on teenagers. I believe that much of this fingerpointing is unwarranted, although hardly surprising. Pop music, which is a blanket term referring to rock, alternative, Top 40, metal, hip-hop, rap, goth and industrial music, has not caused the downfall of Western civilization as predicted by many critics since the mid-1950's; but Americans like quick-fix answers to tough, murky questions, and pop music is an easy scapegoat.

I vividly remember my mom warning me as a young and impressionable second grader that I should not listen to the music of KISS and I should likewise stay away from the kids who carried lunch boxes pasted with this group's frightening clown-like visages. At the time, I had no idea what or who KISS was, but the urgency of my mother's voice served as a warning that I was facing something more evil than I could imagine. KISS went on to achieve immense fame, fortune and misfortune, and recently reunited, with middle-aged paunches and all, as lampoons of their former selves—hardly the type of aural monster Hercules would have encountered on one of his mythic journeys.

Why did my mother feel so strongly about warning me against the dangers of pop music? Perhaps her mother and father had given her the same speech about

Elvis. For three generations, parents have felt the impetus to point their critical fingers at pop music and blame it for every vice St. Paul warned about, with a few more thrown in for good measure. Parents should be concerned about the well-being of their children, but they are fooling themselves if they believe that little Billy will develop more normally if he renounces pop music and instead listens to country and western.

America has been involved in a tense relationship with pop music for at least four decades. In the late 1960's Sharon Tate was murdered by Charles Manson and his group of deranged followers. As this story was being investigated, the press picked up and ran with a phrase that had been written in blood on a wall in Tate's home: "Helter Skelter." Taken from a song on the Beatles' highly praised "White Album," it all at once became the anthem of the Four Horsemen. Similarly, in the mid-80's the heavy metal artists Ozzy Osbourne and Judas Priest were put on trial for supposedly influencing teenagers to kill themselves.

In the wake of the recent high school shootings, pop music again has become a culprit. Shock-rocker Marilyn Manson, and especially this band's namesake front man, were lambasted for inspiring the evil intentions and menacing "goth" lifestyle of the two gun-wielding teenagers. In addition to the fact that Marilyn Manson and goth have nothing to do with each other (mistakenly connecting them betrays the stereotypical musical illiteracy of the older generation), the juxtaposition of pop music with horrible crimes is sad for other reasons as well.

Popular Music's Positive Influences

I have been involved in a love affair with pop music ever since I purchased my first album, Def Leppard's "Pyromania," in 1983. This affair has continued into my four years as a Jesuit, during which time I have played drums in a rock band and written numerous rock CD reviews for a student magazine in Chicago. I do not see a dichotomy between religious life and my musical interests. In fact, through my ministerial experiences as a Jesuit, I have witnessed the hand of God at work through the interaction of teenagers and popular music. In response to the negative press pop music has recently received, I would like to highlight three positive ways popular music can affect teenagers.

> *"For three generations, parents have felt the impetus to point their critical fingers at pop music and blame it for every vice St. Paul warned about."*

Community-building. The teen-age years are a time of transition from childhood to adulthood, and teenagers need to find their own identity apart from their parents and family. This is very normal and healthy, and those readers who are parents should take the time to recall just how difficult it was to gain a foothold on independence during their adolescent years. A very popular way for teenagers to establish independence is by identifying with a group of other teenagers who share their musical interests. Very often, this musical interest is combined with fashion and lifestyle changes that allow the teenagers to feel they are forging their own way toward adulthood without assistance from Mom and Dad. Parents may be disturbed by the musical tastes of their teenagers, but this is to be expected. The music most teenagers listen to in the late 90's is not going to be well received by parents any more than it was in the late 60's. But it serves the same purpose, allowing teenagers to form friendships with peers who share a common interest in a particular music artist or group.

Therapeutic release. Many times, while giving retreats to high school students, I have heard them remark that they will listen to different types of music depending upon their mood. When they are depressed, R.E.M. has just the right song that speaks to them; Ani DiFranco and Tori Amos know what to say to the angry teen-age girl whose boyfriend has just dumped her; Lauryn Hill's infectious grooves are just what the doctor ordered to lighten the spirit on a lonely Friday night; listening to Limp Bizkit after a fight with their parents gives teenagers permission to be angry in a nondestructive way. It is very heartening to witness teenagers turning to music to touch their souls and help them deal with strong emotions because they feel that the music speaks to them in a way that parents, priests or teachers cannot at that moment. Teenagers often associate pop music with special events in their lives, as manifested by the numerous compilation "mix"

> *"Attempting to make a direct correlation between teen-age violence and music is problematic at best."*

tapes many teenagers make by collecting the music that meant a lot to them during a particularly enjoyable summer or while they were involved in a special relationship. Teenagers can use these musical souvenirs to help them recall these enjoyable experiences.

Spirituality. The first two points touched upon aspects of teenagers' spirituality, but I refer here to the use of pop music in a specifically spiritual context, such as a retreat. My experience conducting retreats for teenagers has helped me to understand what a powerful tool pop music can be for tapping into spiritual themes such as darkness/light, death/resurrection and love in a way teenagers can understand and to which they can relate. Pop music can be used at the beginning and end of a retreat talk to provide the proper punctuation to the spiritual matter being conveyed. I am not referring solely to acoustic guitar, bubble-gum lyric pop music, but all types. Since teenagers do invest a lot of time listening to music, building community around music and associating strong emotions with particular music, it is not difficult to bring God into their experience of music. Communicating the power of God's love and companionship by theoretical means to a group of teenagers is not a simple task, but when they can listen to music in a group setting and feel the deep emotions associated with the music, teenagers can be helped to connect their desires and passions with God; and, I hope, God can become more of a real presence in their lives.

Demonizing Music Is Not the Answer

Teenagers who are troubled are going to listen to pop music just as much as teenagers who are not, so attempting to make a direct correlation between teenage violence and music is problematic at best. Pop music is not predicted as an agent of mass destruction in the Book of Revelation, and Marilyn Manson is no more responsible for the Littleton shootings than Joan Osborne's sappy oeuvre "(What if God was) One of Us" is responsible for effecting mass conversions to deism. Teenagers are going through difficult transitions and definitely need guidance from their elders, but demonizing the music they listen to is not a constructive way to provide support.

The Effects of Violent Video Games on Children Are Exaggerated

by Gary Chapman

About the author: *Gary Chapman is director of the 21st Century Project at the University of Texas at Austin and the author of a biweekly column for the* Los Angeles Times *entitled "Digital Nation."*

The tragedy . . . in Littleton, Colorado, is still on the minds of Americans, polls show, no doubt reinforced by [the May 1999] school shootings in Georgia. Events such as these could bring widespread censorship to the Internet, at least in the United States, and also, possibly, restraints on video and computer games.

The Search for a Scapegoat

Vice President Al Gore called a news conference shortly after the Colorado killings to announce support for parental controls on children's use of the Internet. The Federal Communications Commission is reportedly mulling over a rule that would require Internet service providers to offer free filtering software to their customers. There has also been new attention directed at violent video and computer games.

The American tendency to blame possible but speculative influences on the perpetrators of horrendous crimes has become a familiar pattern.

First, the potential negative influences are identified by minute examination of the criminal's life history. Second, factors that are already considered problematic or repulsive are given special emphasis. Third, the prevalence of these influences is assigned to the neglect or mendacity of a particular political persuasion, such as when former House Speaker Newt Gingrich blamed the shooting at Columbine High School in Colorado on "liberals." Fourth, defenders of the scapegoated influence point out that millions of people are exposed to the same influence but do not become criminals. Finally, the spike in public attention and concern reaches a point where politicians feel they must do something.

Needless to say, this is a spectacularly unsophisticated and almost rube-like way to address a problem and, in the case of school violence, there may not even be a problem because schools are far safer places, statistically, than streets or even homes. And when the remedy contemplated is some form of censorship, this threatens to shape the experience of everyone in society even though the crime was committed by only a handful of people.

Violence Is a Male Problem

A concession that seemed curiously missing in all the talk after the Columbine High tragedy is that the problem with violence in our society—including "virtual" violence—is almost exclusively a problem of males, especially young men and boys. Girls tend not to enjoy violent video games; girls don't usually access Web sites dedicated to ethnic or racial hatred; girls almost never shoot up a school or anywhere else.

So if we are to focus on the problem of violence, we need to address only half of the population, not the entire population, as probable or potential sources of violence. Then we have to admit that most boys and men are not violent, even those who play violent video games or who own guns or who enjoy violent action movies.

What makes some males violent? We're not sure, but some experts believe it is a transition from fantasy to action that is rooted in shame, anger, fear and a lack of connection to others. Author William Pollack, in his best-selling book "Real Boys," writes: "I do not believe that a boy who feels truly connected and loved and who

"We need a far more sophisticated discussion about the link between simulated violence and real violence."

has safe settings where he can express his emotions will be motivated to violence by exposure to violence in the media."

Pollack recommends ways for parents to encourage their boys to share their feelings and for parents to avoid the common practice of encouraging stoicism, toughness and "manly" qualities in boys at a young age.

Christina Hoff Sommers, a fellow at the American Enterprise Institute in Washington, is writing a book called "The War Against Boys," and she disagrees with Pollack. "There is no evidence," she said, "that being able to express your emotions leads to mental health." She calls Pollack's diagnosis the "clinical fallacy," an attempt to "pathologize all boys." She says, "What Pollack wants to do is to make boys more like girls."

Sommers instead recommends rigorous training in character and ethics. "To get to the heart of the problem, you have to go to ethics in the schools—there's been a move away from teaching right and wrong, both in the schools and in the home," she says. "Boys need this more than girls," she adds.

80

Violent Video Games Are Not the Real Problem

What is the role of computer games or the Internet?

Pollack and Sommers agree that violent video games or violence in the media can desensitize some boys to violence.

The key to violence is anger and shame, combined with lack of character and ethical development. Computers may actually feed this if a boy, who is angry, shamed and withdrawn into a fantasy world of revenge, is allowed to spend hours alone on a computer with a virtual means of enhancing his revenge fantasy, such as playing a "first-person shooter" simulation game of murder and mayhem. The Internet may contribute to this too if the boy is seeking sites that reinforce his anger instead of challenging or diverting it into something more productive.

There are some, like Sommers, who think we should err on the side of caution and either pass "reasonable" legislation or, as she put it, "shame" the computer game makers into pulling violent video games from stores. That attitude usually extends to Internet filtering software, too. Others think the attraction of males to action and violence is so overwhelming that it's impossible to regulate or control, and that we'd do better to concentrate on the tiny number of boys and men who veer into violent or pathological behavior. Still others point out that the major problem is the availability of guns, which can make violence much more lethal to its victims.

In general, we need a far more sophisticated discussion about the link between simulated violence and real violence. We also need to be cautious about the blunt instrument of government censorship—something that affects everyone—when the actual source of vexation is a small population of boys and men whose real problems are not principally exposure to violent games or the Internet.

Teenagers Are Not Becoming More Violent

by Mike Males

About the author: *Mike Males is the author of* The Scapegoat Generation: America's War on Adolescents *and* Framing Youth: 10 Myths About the Next Generation.

Two weeks after the school massacre in Littleton, Colorado, anguished parents in a California suburb where murder is also rare found such tragedy "can happen here." A 39-year-old man drove his Cadillac into a crowded preschool playground in Costa Mesa, killing a 3-year-old and a 4-year-old, leaving two small children in critical condition and injuring two more toddlers and an adult aide. His motive seemed to be incomprehensible rage: The driver was quoted by police as remorselessly seeking to execute "innocent children" because of a former girlfriend's rejection.

But while the shootings in Littleton and schools around the nation have been cited as a horrific sign of America's social breakdown, Costa Mesa's tragedy was not used as a metaphor for apocalyptic social collapse by political leaders and scholarly authorities.

Why? Because, like other adults who commit mass killings, the Costa Mesa killer is viewed as an individual psychopath, representative only of his isolated rage. The commentators who magnify a teenage gunman into a poster child for "youth culture" gone terribly awry do not similarly portray a grown-up who commits atrocity as reflecting a diseased "middle-age culture."

Adults Are Far More Violent than Teenagers

As another White House summit on youth and school violence starts, the reasons for the national panic over kids killing kids, versus the virtual ignoring of the far-more-common phenomenon of adults killing kids, raise sobering questions about the attitudes of authorities—and Americans, in general—toward young people. Why do occasional killings by students generate commentary demonizing a generation of young people, when the more prevalent killings by

Reprinted from "Why Demonize a Healthy Teen Culture?" by Mike Males, *Los Angeles Times,* May 9, 1999. Reprinted with permission from the author.

adults draw no similar fears of widespread grown-up pathology?

Here is the baffling paradox: While student shootings remain rare, rage killings by middle-aged adults, a group criminologists insist has mellowed out of its violent years, are epidemic. [Since 1997] in Southern California alone, seemingly solid, middle-class, midlife adults committed a dozen massacres—a bus yard of workers raked with assault-rifle barrage, an office filled with semi-automatic pistol fire, children gunned as they fled down a pastoral suburban lane—that left 40 dead, including 16 children.

Recent trends provide ample reason to view this inexplicable blood spilling by middle-aged adults of comfortable background as part of a larger, alarming reality. Drug abuse, family violence and breakup, felony arrest and imprisonment have exploded among adults age 30 to 50, the parent generation whose values are extolled by many. Defying every crime theory, felony arrests of white adults older

> *"Rates of murder, school violence, drug abuse, criminal arrest, violent death and gun fatality among middle- and upper-class teenagers have declined."*

than 30, California's fastest-rising criminal and prisoner population, have tripled, from 31,000 in 1975 to 106,000 in 1997.

This raises a second paradox: Today's middle-class and suburban teenagers are better behaved than kids of the past. Regardless of what dire theory of societal unraveling experts use to explain why two suburban Colorado teens went on a murderous rampage, a major fact is overlooked: The best evidence shows that rates of murder, school violence, drug abuse, criminal arrest, violent death and gun fatality among middle- and upper-class teenagers have declined over the last 15 to 30 years.

This is especially true in California. Compared with their counterparts of the 1970s, white teenagers of the late 1990s show sharply lower per-person rates of gun deaths (down 25%), suicide (down 30%), murder arrest (down 30%), criminal arrest (down 50%), drug abuse (overdose deaths down 80%) and violent fatality of all kinds (down an incredible 45% in the last decade). Nationally, surveys show 90% of today's teens are happy and feel good about themselves; 80% get along well with their parents and other adults; more young people volunteer for charities and services than ever; and parents, religion and teachers are the biggest influences on youth.

Pop Culture Should Not Be Demonized

With such statistics, it is hard to justify the widespread belief that today's adolescents are alienated, angst-ridden and troubled. If pop culture, music, video games and Internet images affect teenagers, we should credit them for the fact that young people are behaving better. In fact, it may be that young people's bewildering array of informal, "alternative families"—ravers, Goths, posses, 'zine cultures, Internet forums, gay and lesbian groups, skateboarders, gay and lesbian skateboarder 'zinesters—help insulate them from the difficulties of increasingly chaotic biological families and account for the surprising good health of youths who should be most at risk.

The shootings in Littleton and other schools are not part of a larger trend toward more student and school violence, but tragic aberrations. The political and professional theorists whose explanations for Littleton flooded the media and policy forums displayed a singular failure to get a grip. Twenty-five million teenagers attend 20,000 schools nationwide. Ten students in seven schools committed the widely-publicized shootings of the past 18 months. Teenage gunners are not representatives of all teens, even alienated, outcast ones, but are rare, extremely disturbed individuals. There is no evidence that adolescents are more troubled than adults or any more disturbed today than they ever were. As psychologist Laura Berk's 1997 text, "Child Development," notes, "the overall rate of severe psychological disturbance rises only slightly (by 2%) from childhood to adolescence, when it is the same as in the adult population—about 15% or 20%."

But to say that murderous rage is rare and declining among middle-class and affluent youth does not mean its prevalence is zero. Teenagers are subject to the same environments and pressures that drive some adults to violence, and teens inhabit the same adult society whose infestation of superlethal firearms too easily converts anger into slaughter. Exaggerating rare instances of teenage rage into some kind of generation-wide craziness not only inflicts unwarranted paranoia, blanket surveillance, draconian restrictions and harmful interference with normal growing up on a generally healthy generation of young people, it also severely hampers investigation into identifying and forestalling the narrow, individual psychoses that produce rage killers of all ages.

The baseless panic about young people inflamed by so many politicians, leading psychologists, pundits and institutional scholars is more damaging to our social fabric than the isolated teenage murders they seize upon. Ignoring clear statistics and research, authorities seem to lie in wait for suburban youth killings, months and thousands of miles apart, to validate a false hypothesis of generational disease, even as they ignore more compelling evidence of deteriorating adult behavior.

> *"If pop culture, music, video games and Internet images affect teenagers, we should credit them for the fact that young people are behaving better."*

This subversion of health and safety goals to politically warped, crowd-pleasing nostrums about "saving our kids" endangers kids in reality and helps perpetuate America's dismal reputation as the deadliest, most bullet-riddled, unhealthiest nation in the Western world.

Chapter 3

Should Children's Access to Violent Media Be Restricted?

Chapter Preface

In the debate over media violence, a common view is that children are more affected by such material than are adults. Adults, the reasoning goes, have the right to enjoy whatever television programs, movies, music, or video games they choose—and are presumed responsible enough to view violence without becoming violent themselves. But children are thought to be much more impressionable. Those who hold this view believe parents have the right—and the responsibility—to limit their children's exposure to media violence.

In fact, increased parental responsibility is one of the most commonly posed solutions to the problem of media violence. John Romano, producer of NBC's program *Third Watch*, sums it up this way: "If you don't want your kids watching, turn the darn thing [TV] off."

But many parents say that this is a simplistic response to a complex problem. Of course parents have a responsibility to monitor their children's television habits, they argue, but the government and the television industry should also do what they can to help parents. In response to this argument, Congress passed the Telecommunications Act of 1996. Among other provisions, the act required television broadcasters to develop a ratings system for TV programs. The act also required that by the year 2000 television manufacturers include the V-chip, an electronic device that allows parents to block out any program with a particular rating, in all new television sets. Dick Rolfe, president of the antiviolence Dove Foundation, writes that the V-chip simply "empowers parents to do their jobs more effectively."

The V-chip legislation has met with its share of controversy, however. Many critics have attacked it as an incomplete solution to the problem: "[The legislation] presupposes that parents will accept the responsibility of monitoring their children's choice of shows," notes writer Ron Sabey. "What about the children in families where parents don't care or don't take responsibility?" Still others argue that the V-chip and TV ratings system go too far and are a threat to free speech. "Once the v-chip is in place," writes Solveig Bernstein of the libertarian Cato Institute, "nothing stops government from using informal pressures to approve or disapprove ratings. . . . As the winds of politics shift, . . . perhaps v-chips will be used to block negative political advertising, alcohol ads, or diaper advertising."

The debate over the V-chip shows how eager many groups are for government assistance in limiting children's exposure to media violence, and how fiercely opposed others are to any government initiative that may threaten free speech. In the following chapter, authors debate other methods by which parents, the entertainment industry, and the government might restrict children's access to violent media.

The Entertainment Industry Should Reduce Its Production of Youth-Oriented Violent Media

by Media Appeal

About the author: *Media Appeal is a group of prominent Americans and other concerned citizens who have called upon the entertainment industry to establish a voluntary code of conduct regarding media violence.*

Editor's note: The following is Media Appeal's "Appeal to Hollywood," the organization's ongoing petition to the entertainment industry. The petition has been signed by dozens of academics, leaders in the entertainment industry, and Republican and Democratic politicians, including former presidents Jimmy Carter and Gerald Ford. The petition first began circulating in mid-1999 and has been signed by over ten thousand people. Individuals can sign the petition via the web at www.media-appeal.org.

American parents today are deeply worried about their children's exposure to an increasingly toxic popular culture. Events in Littleton, Colorado, are only the most recent reminder that something is deeply amiss in our media age. Violence and explicit sexual content in television, films, music, and video games have escalated sharply in recent years. Children of all ages are now being exposed to a barrage of images and words that threaten not only to rob them of normal childhood innocence, but also to distort their view of reality and even undermine their character growth.

These concerns know no political or partisan boundaries. According to a recent CNN-USA Today-Gallup poll, 76 percent of adults agree that TV, movies, and popular music are negative influences on children. Seventy-five percent report that they make efforts to protect children from such harmful influences.

Nearly the same number—73 percent—say shielding children from the negative influences of today's media culture is "nearly impossible."

Moreover, there is a growing public appreciation of the link between our excessively violent and degrading entertainment culture and the horrifying new crimes we see emerging among our young: schoolchildren gunning down their teachers and fellow students en masse, killing sprees inspired by self-indulgently violent films, teenagers murdering their babies only to return to dance at the prom.

Media Violence Is Only Part of a Larger Problem

Clearly, there is no simple causation at work here. Many factors are contributing to the crisis engulfing many of our children—negligent parenting, ineffective schools, divorce and family disintegration, and the ready availability of firearms. All are important, and all should be a part of our national conversation on this problem. But surely no one can argue that our entertainment culture should be exempt from the discussion.

Among researchers, the proposition that entertainment violence adversely influences attitudes and behavior is no longer controversial; there is overwhelming evidence of its harmful effects. Numerous studies show that degrading images of violence and sex have a desensitizing effect. Nowhere is the threat greater than to our at-risk youth—youngsters whose broken homes or disadvantaged environments make them acutely susceptible to acting upon impulses shaped by violent and dehumanizing media imagery.

Many factors, including the drive for profit in an increasingly competitive media marketplace, are contributing to the downward spiral in entertainment and the disappearance of even minimum standards.

In the past, the entertainment industry was more conscious of its unique responsibility for the health of our culture. For thirty years, television broadcasters lived by the National Association of Broadcasters (NAB) Television Code, which detailed broadcasters' responsibilities to the community, to children, and to society and prescribed specific standards. For many years this voluntary code set boundaries that enabled television to thrive as a creative medium without causing undue damage to the bedrock values of our society.

> *"We call upon industry leaders in all media—television, film, music, video, and electronic games—to band together to develop a new voluntary code of conduct."*

In recent years, several top entertainment executives have spoken out, laudably, on the need for minimum standards and, more recently, on the desirability of more family-friendly programming. But to effect real change, these individual expressions must be translated into a new, collective affirmation of social responsibility on the part of the media industry as a whole.

As parents all of us, too, have a major responsibility to supervise our children's access to the entertainment media—be it television, films, music, videos, video games, or the Internet. Allowing children unsupervised access to today's media is the moral equivalent of letting them go play on the freeway. Parents should limit TV viewing hours. They should know what programs their child is watching, what music he or she is listening to, what films he or she is attending, what videos he or she is renting, what video games he or she is playing, and what web sites he or she is surfing on the Internet.

While most parents are concerned about the media's influence, some, unfortunately, neglect these critical obligations. But today even the most conscientious parent cries out for help from an industry that too often abdicates its responsibility for its powerful impact on the young.

An Appeal to Hollywood

Therefore we, the undersigned, call upon executives of the media industry—as well as CEOs of companies that advertise in the electronic media—to join with us, and with America's parents, in a new social compact aimed at renewing our culture and making our media environment more healthy for our society and safer for our children.

We call upon industry leaders in all media—television, film, music, video, and electronic games—to band together to develop a new voluntary code of conduct, broadly modeled on the NAB code.

The code we envision would (1) affirm in clear terms the industry's vital responsibilities for the health of our culture; (2) establish certain minimum standards for violent, sexual, and degrading material for each medium, below which producers can be expected not to go; (3) commit the industry to an overall reduction in the level of entertainment violence; (4) ban the practice of targeting adult-oriented entertainment to youth markets; (5) provide for more accurate information to parents on media content while committing to the creation of "windows" or "safe havens" for family programming (including a revival of TV's "Family Hour"); and, finally, (6) pledge the industry to significantly greater creative efforts to develop good family-oriented entertainment.

We strongly urge parents to express their support for a new voluntary code of conduct directly to media executives and advertisers, whether through calls, letters, faxes, or e-mails, or by becoming signers of this Appeal by filling out and submitting the form below. And we call upon all parents to fulfill their part of the compact by responsibly supervising their children's media exposure.

We are not advocating censorship or wholesale strictures on artistic creativity. We are not demanding that all entertainment be geared to young children. Finally, we are not asking government to police the media. Rather, we are asking the entertainment industry to assume a decent minimum of responsibility for its own actions and to take some modest steps of self-restraint. And we are asking parents to help in this task, not just by taking responsibility for shielding their own children, but also by making their concerns known to media executives and advertisers.

Hollywood has an enormous influence on America, particularly the young. By making a concerted effort to turn its energies to promoting decent, shared values and strengthening American families, the entertainment industry has it within its power to help make an America worthy of the Third Millennium. We, leaders from government, the religious community, the nonprofit world, and the private sector—and members of the entertainment community—challenge the entertainment industry to this great task. We appeal to those who are reaping great profits to give something back. We believe that by choosing to do good, the entertainment industry can also make good—and both the industry and our society will be richer and better as a result.

> *"We are asking the entertainment industry to assume a decent minimum of responsibility for its own actions and to take some modest steps of self-restraint."*

The Entertainment Industry Should Not Be Allowed to Market Violent Media to Children

by Orrin G. Hatch

About the author: *Orrin Hatch is a Republican senator from Utah.*

Editor's note: The following viewpoint is excerpted from Hatch's May 1999 testimony before the Senate Committee on Commerce, Science, and Transportation, at a hearing entitled Marketing Violence to Children.

There is a sense among many Americans that we are powerless to change our culture and that this feeling of powerlessness has restrained our ambition for solutions in the wake of the Littleton tragedy. As Dr. William Bennett said recently on a national talk show, if the two students who committed the murders at Columbine High had "carried Bibles and [said] Hail the Prince of Peace and King of Kings, they would have been hauled into the principal's office." Instead, they saluted Hitler and were ignored. Ironically, it seems the only time we tolerate prayer in school these days is when people come to on-school memorials in the wake of tragedies.

Holding the Entertainment Industry Accountable

If the murder of twelve innocent students and one teacher cannot give us the strength to shed this defeatism, then we are doomed to see more tragedies. I believe that we can change our culture if only we are willing to lead. The time has come for us as a nation to demand more accountability from everyone involved—including the entertainment industry.

Some of you may know that, in recent years, I have taken to writing inspirational music. My hope is that perhaps just one person will hear my music and

Testimony given by Senator Orrin G. Hatch before the Senate Committee on Commerce, Science, and Transportation, May 4, 1999.

be inspired to right a wrong or lead a more religious life. In short, I believe that music and popular culture can be a tremendous force for good. For example, take the film *Schindler's List.* I believe that this one movie did more to educate a new generation of Americans about the inhumanity, and the occasional acts of courage and compassion, of the Holocaust than any high school history course could.

So, I do not come here to attack Hollywood or the entertainment industry. Indeed, this is just one part of a much more complex problem. But I do hope that we can encourage the industry to work with us to do what is best for our children. Why can't

> *"Why should . . . violent video games—games the industry itself has found unsuitable for children—be advertised and marketed to children?"*

this industry, which is a source for so much good in America, do more to discourage the production and marketing of filth to children. Why shouldn't the industry help fight the marketing of violence to young people?

The tragedy in Littleton was a bizarre and complex crime. We should examine this and other school shootings from every angle and not single-out one potential cause before we know all the facts. Every serious explanation should be considered. Nevertheless, as the *New York Times* noted in its Friday [April 30, 1999] editorial, "the search for the cause in the Littleton shootings continues, and much of it has come to focus on violent video games."

Indeed, studies have indicated that prolonged exposure of children to ultra-violent movies and video games increases the likelihood for aggression. As President Clinton noted in his radio address last week, the two juveniles who committed the atrocities in Littleton played the ultra-violent video game Doom obsessively. In addition, the 14-year-old boy who killed three in the Paducah, Kentucky, school killing was an avid video game player. In fact, the juvenile had never fired a pistol before he shot eight classmates that terrible day in 1997.

The Marketing of Violent Video Games

Given that there is evidence that extremely violent movies, music, and video games have negative effects on children, we must be concerned about how these products are marketed and sold. According to the National Institute on Media and the Family, some manufacturers of video and computer games are marketing ultra-violent video games rated for adults only to children. In 1998, the National Institute on Media and the Family conducted a thorough study of the video and computer game industry. Some of the findings were disturbing. For example, lurid advertisements for violent video games are aimed directly at children. The advertisement for the video game Destrega states: "Let the slaughter begin," while the advertisement for the video game Carmageddon states: "As easy as killing babies with axes." And as Senator Brownback noted last week on the Senate floor, the advertisement for the game "Quake" states:

"Blowing your friends to pieces with a rocket launcher is only the beginning."

These and similar advertisements appeared in recent gaming magazines which are targeted to teenagers. Moreover, an advertisement for Resident Evil 2, a violent video game rated for adults only, was featured in the magazine *Sports Illustrated for Kids.* Few people would argue that cigarettes, alcohol, or X-rated or NC-17 rated movies should be advertised in children's magazines. Why should such violent video games—games the industry itself has found unsuitable for children—be advertised and marketed to children?

In response to a series of hearings in the Senate Judiciary Committee in 1993 and 1994, the video game industry adopted a thorough and independent rating system of video games. Industry compliance with the rating system is high. Fairness dictates that these positive steps be noted. Yet, despite such a comprehensive rating system, there is little evidence that such ratings are enforced or even taken seriously.

For example, last year, the National Institute on Media and the Family found that despite such a voluntary rating system for video games, only 21 percent of retail and rental stores had any policies prohibiting the sale or rental of mature games to minors. Just this weekend, less than ten days after the Columbine massacre, a twelve-year-old boy bought the video games "Doom" and "Quake"—both of which are rated for adults only—without even a question from a local Washington area retail store. In fact, this particular ultra-violent game was actually recommended to the twelve-year-old child by the store's clerks. As the boy later observed, "I could have bought anything in the store if I'd had enough money."

Violent and Misogynistic Music

Nor is the problem of marketing violence to children limited to video games. In recent years, the lyrics of popular music have grown more violent and depraved. And much of the violence and cruelty in modern music is directed toward women. As Senator Brownback noted on the Senate floor last week, the group Nine Inch Nails had a commercial success a few years ago with a song celebrating the rape and murder of a woman. This is not an isolated example. Hatred and violence against women in mainstream hip-hop and alternative music are widespread and unmistakable. Consider the singer Marilyn Manson, whom MTV named the "Best New Artist of the Year" last year. Some of Manson's less vulgar lyrics include: "Who says date rape isn't kind?"; "Let's just kill everyone and let your god sort them out"; and "the housewife I will beat, the prolife I will kill." Other Manson lyrics cannot be repeated here. Again this weekend, a twelve-year-old boy bought a Marilyn Manson compact disc from a local Washington area record store, even though it was rated for adult content. Ironically, the warning label on the disc was covered by the price tag, which signals to me that these record warnings are not taken seriously. Or consider Eminem, the hip-hop artist featured frequently on MTV who recently wrote

93

"Bonnie and Clyde"—a song in which he described his killing his child's mother and dumping her body into the ocean.

Despite historic, bipartisan legislation by the state and federal governments, it is stunning how much modern music glorifies acts of violence, sexual and otherwise, against women. This music is what many children are listening to. This music is marketed to our youth. We should not ignore the fact that violent, misogynistic music may ultimately affect the behavior and attitudes of many young men toward women. One might argue that these groups are not embraced by the entertainment industry. How then would the industry explain a 1998 Grammy nomination for Nine Inch Nails and a 1999 Grammy nomination for Marilyn Manson? It is one thing to say these people can't produce this material, it's another thing for the industry to embrace it.

Justified Outrage

Many Americans were justifiably outraged when it was discovered that tobacco companies marketed cigarettes to children. I believe that we should be equally concerned if we find that violent music and video games are being marketed to children. Senator Lieberman and I have recently considered asking the Federal Trade Commission or the Department of Justice to investigate the marketing practices of the video-game, music, and movie industry. Such an investigation could determine the extent of this problem and provide possible solutions. In addition, I have begun discussions with Internet Service Providers and computer manufacturers about how to make screening software, which helps parents protect their children from inappropriate material on the Internet, more readily available.

> *"Limiting access of ultra-violent music and video games to children does not raise the same constitutional concerns that a general prohibition on such material would entail."*

Limiting access of ultra-violent music and video games to children does not raise the same constitutional concerns that a general prohibition on such material would entail. For example, while some can reasonably contend that the First Amendment protects certain X-rated material, no one can reasonably argue that the Constitution prohibits restricting such material to children. Consequently, I have prepared an amendment to be offered on the Senate floor . . . that would direct the Administration to investigate the marketing of violent music and video games to children. In addition, I am considering an enforcement mechanism for the current ratings system.

Parents Should Limit Children's Exposure to Violence in the Media

by Madeline Levine

About the author: *Madeline Levine is a clinical psychologist, the mother of three sons, and the author of* See No Evil: A Guide to Protecting Our Children from Media Violence.

A mother and her 3-year-old son walk briskly into their local movie theater for an afternoon showing of *Snow White and the Seven Dwarfs.* They settle into their seats just as the lights go down. The mother can feel her young son's body stiffen in the darkness. Midway through the movie, a menacing, hooded figure with long, blood-red fingernails appears on the screen and cackles at her reflection in the mirror. The little boy closes his eyes in fear, and as the sinister music builds, lets out a terrified scream. The manager hurries over and offers a prompt refund to the embarrassed mother and sobbing child.

That mother is me, and the child is my youngest son, proof that even a psychologist who has spent more than 16 years working with children can make mistakes about what is too scary for her own kids. There is a very good reason why grown-ups make mistakes: What is disturbing to children, especially preschoolers, often comes as a surprise to adults.

Screen Violence Is Inappropriate for Preschoolers

Preschool children (ages 3, 4, and 5) inhabit a world that is magical, unique, and quite distinct from that of grown-ups, teenagers, or even older children. Disney makes many wonderful movies that children enjoy and watch over and over again. So why did my 3-year-old fall apart? The answer lies in the "appearance-reality distinction."

Studies have looked at children at different ages to determine whether they can distinguish between what is real and what only appears to be real. For instance, researchers took a red toy car and covered it with a green filter that made it appear to be black. Despite extensive explanations about the difference between what something looks like and what it "really and truly is," the 3-year-olds continued to say, when asked what color the car was, that it was black.

Just as the researchers couldn't convince the children that what they saw wasn't real, no amount of reassurance from you—"It's just a movie, honey. It's not real"—will convince your preschooler that Snow White's stepmother is just pretend. Of course, not all young children will react as my son did, but until they can grasp this distinction—which is usually around the age of 6—it's best to protect your kids from even the most outlandishly unrealistic portrayals of bad people.

> *"It's best to protect your kids [under the age of 6] from even the most outlandishly unrealistic portrayals of bad people."*

You may wonder why you can read your preschooler fairy tales like "Little Red Riding Hood" with no ill effects. In this at-times gruesome tale, a grandmother is eaten alive by a wolf. Your child may be somewhat anxious while listening to this story. But there's a big difference between reading a book and seeing a movie. Reading or being read to allows the child to conjure up the exact amount of scariness that she can handle.

When choosing movies or television programs for children under 6, you should be aware that kids this age are particularly scared of things that change suddenly from the ordinary to the grotesque. Researchers at the University of Wisconsin, Madison, have found that preschoolers are far more disturbed by David Banner's transformation into the Incredible Hulk than by the movie *Jaws*.

On the other hand, much of what we think will frighten preschoolers is often less upsetting than expected. News broadcasts are a good example. While the graphic photographs and footage are certainly troubling, the news is primarily verbal, and young children are less attentive, and therefore less vulnerable, to what they hear.

Realistic Portrayals of Violence Are More Frightening to Older Children

After the whirlwind pace of the preschool years, parents often allow themselves to relax a bit. But it is not true that as children grow up they are less susceptible to being frightened by the media; it is simply that what frightens them changes. No longer terrified of monsters and goblins, children 6 and over are more fearful of injury and abandonment.

Realistic movies in which a young child is the victim of abuse and exploitation, or in which grown-ups inadequately perform their role as protectors of the young, are far more damaging for kids 6 and over than movies that are clearly based in fantasy.

Jurassic Park, rated PG-13, was frightening to a broad range of kids for very different reasons. The 3-, 4-, and 5-year-olds were scared by the violent dinosaurs. However, to the 6- and 7-year-olds, the fact that it was adults who jeopardized the children's safety was much more disturbing than the creatures themselves.

Children 6 and over are less apt to be frightened by movies such as *Star Trek* and *Star Wars,* which are obviously make-believe. The lack of realism helps these children feel distanced from what they are watching.

By 8 or 9 years old, children are capable of understanding that television and movies are largely fabrications—the workings of people's imaginations. At this point, news reporting about violence, because of its factual nature, can be particularly disturbing to them.

The story of Polly Klaas illustrates how terrifying the news can be when children identify with the victim. On October 1, 1993, 12-year-old Polly was enjoying a sleep-over party with two girlfriends when she was kidnapped from her suburban home in Petaluma, California. She was abducted from her bedroom while her mother slept in the next room, a detail that made this a particularly disturbing crime for children. Polly's smiling face became a staple on news programs. When she was discovered dead several months later, news broadcasts juxtaposed footage of her laughing and dancing on home videotape with that of her covered body found off a highway.

> *"Although kids do need to be warned of dangers, exposing them to disturbing images does not make them more capable of dealing with such dangers."*

A study at Stanford University, led by psychiatrist Sara Stein, M.D., looked at the effects of the media coverage of this crime on children. More than 1,100 children, ages 8 to 18, in three different states were studied. Over 80 percent reported that they "sometimes" or "often" were bothered by symptoms such as bad dreams or intrusive thoughts that they could not control. Not surprisingly, the younger children (because of their inability to distance themselves) and the girls (because of their identification) showed more symptoms of being disturbed by the news reports than did the older children and the boys.

In my own practice, which was not far from the kidnapping, I saw several 8- and 9-year-old girls who exhibited symptoms of post-traumatic stress disorder following Polly's kidnapping and murder. Previously healthy children, they reported sleep disturbances, concentration problems, and anxiety. One girl slept with a baseball bat next to her bed; another refused to sleep near a window.

Parents Have a Duty to Protect Children from Harm

Although kids do need to be warned of dangers, exposing them to disturbing images does not make them more capable of dealing with such dangers. On the contrary, it traumatizes them and ultimately makes them less competent.

One of the major responsibilities of child rearing is to foster independence while protecting kids from harm: "Yes, you can walk to the store with your sister, but you have to hold her hand when you cross the street." "You can ride your bike in the park, but not on the road." "I will let you see some movies, but not *Batman*. It's too scary for little kids." By learning more about the movies and television programs your children watch and by considering their level of maturity, you can "dose" the world for them, steering them toward films and shows that won't make them more afraid, but will expand their horizons and aid their development.

Better Ratings Systems Would Help Parents Protect Children from Media Violence

by Michael Medved

About the author: *Michael Medved, formerly chief film critic for the* New York Post *and cohost of the television program* Sneak Previews, *is a radio talk show host and columnist for* USA Today. *His books include* Hollywood vs. America *and* Saving Childhood: Protecting Our Children from the National Assault on Innocence.

Editor's note: The following viewpoint was given in May 1999 as testimony before the House of Representatives Judiciary Committee on Youth Culture and Violence.

After all the anguished conversation about media violence in the last three weeks—the Congressional hearings, the entertainment "summit conferences," the probing TV specials, and the solemn pronouncements of politicians—will we once again shrug our shoulders, change the subject, and do nothing? Americans of every political persuasion have reached an overwhelming consensus that brutality in the popular culture exerts a destructive influence on the attitudes and behavior of our kids. Is it enough to respond to this consensus by stating the obvious: that the chief responsibility for protecting the young from damaging ultimately falls upon their parents?

No, it is not enough—especially when the entertainment industry itself could easily seize this unique opportunity to make one obvious, immensely important reform to help parents cope with the media onslaught.

We desperately need a universal rating system to cover all elements of pop culture—a clear, consistent means of labeling movies, television, CDs and video games so that consumers can make more informed choices in the marketplace.

Testimony given by Michael Medved before the House of Representatives Judiciary Committee on Youth Culture and Violence, May 13, 1999.

Even Hollywood's most shameless apologists must face the fact that the current situation with ratings and parental warnings amounts to a chaotic, incomprehensible mess. Sure, a typical parent may have some idea what the Motion Picture Association means by designating a given film as "PG-13." But how many among us could even begin to explain the television rating of "TV-Y7" or "TV-MA"? And does anyone out there in the real world fully grasp video game ratings of "M" or "AO"?

Continued confusion is not only unnecessary; it is indefensible. Leaders of the various media—who, after all, often represent the same huge parent companies like Warner Brothers or Disney—should come together to clear away all the puzzling abbreviations and contradictory standards. The movie ratings— "G," "PG," "PG-13," "R," and "NC-17"—should provide the basis for a new across-the-board system that offers parents with far more meaningful guidance. That guidance will be particularly important when, in the near future, most TV sets will be equipped with a V-chip, a device that is only as useful and usable as the ratings the industry provides.

> *"The current situation with ratings and parental warnings amounts to a chaotic, incomprehensible mess."*

During informal conversations, both network and movie studio executives displayed a positive and open-minded response to the notion of creating consistent ratings for all media. Establishing one unified system with recognizable abbreviations seems, in fact, particularly appropriate at a time when the big entertainment companies are trying to emphasize "synergy" and "convergence" in their multi-faceted operations.

The movie industry began rating its releases more than 30 years ago, so its designations are far more familiar to the public than the new categories established in other areas of entertainment. Of course, there are subtle distinctions between a television rating of "TV-14" and a film label of "PG-13," but are these differences important enough to justify perpetuating the current muddle? Surveys show that few parents make use of the new TV ratings—in part because so few understand them.

Establishing a universal rating would both facilitate and encourage greater parental supervision in the entertainment that children consume. At the moment, the only information provided about music releases, for instance, is an all-purpose advisory affixed to CDs and tapes that warns of "explicit content." This is an all-or-nothing categorization that gives adults little information or assistance in understanding the nature of the usually unfamiliar titles their children may purchase. Many parents would feel grateful for some guidance as to which releases might qualify as "PG" or "PG-13," and which have earned an "R." At the moment, albums only get tagged if they are, in effect, "NC-17."

None of this amounts to censorship of any kind, nor would it require governmental intervention. The universal ratings, like the well-established system for feature films, would remain entirely voluntary. If consumers choose to ignore it, they remain totally free to do so.

Of course, some ratings decisions for specific TV shows or musical releases or video games will seem capricious and illogical—that's certainly been the case with some controversial movie designations in the past. But even imperfect efforts to provide parents with more adequate guidance would serve to empower them.

Nor should anyone argue that consistent, comprehensible across-the-board ratings would inevitably lead to more emphasis on racy material—with producers trying to maximize their revenues by going for the harsher, hipper, more popular "R" designation. In movies, producers appeal decisions of the ratings board all the time—but always to get the softer rating, not the harder one. They have recognized for years now that "PG" titles fare, on average, far better than "R" titles precisely because they appeal to a broader audience. Some movies— like "Saving Private Ryan," for instance—require an "R" for their creative purposes, and find a huge audience in spite of it. The same will prove true for some video games, musical albums and TV shows.

But at least a universal system that the public understands will make it harder to market graphically violent material to unsuspecting kids or to pass it off as "family fare." An "R" rating may not keep all customers away from a piece of popular entertainment, but at least it serves as fair warning.

In recent years, the people's entertainment preferences proved that many Americans mean what they say when they demand more wholesome alternatives. The new industry-wide ratings system would help them find what they're seeking. Jack Valenti, President of the Motion Picture Association, industry elder statesman and the godfather of the well-known movie ratings, might well be enlisted to spearhead this new effort. At the very least, it would amount to a good faith response to the unmistakable public concern. If the potentates of popular culture feel sincerely worried over disturbing messages reaching our kids, then why should they resist this moderate, common-sense step? It involves no new restrictions; just new information—new tools many families will choose to use. Few parents expect government bureaucrats or entertainment executives to take their

> *"Establishing a universal rating would both facilitate and encourage greater parental supervision in the entertainment that children consume."*

places when it comes to guiding entertainment choices of their kids. Yet it shouldn't be too much to ask of media moguls if, to paraphrase Winston Churchill, they would "give us the tools, and we shall finish the job."

Restricting Children's Access to Violent Media Would Be Censorship

by Free Expression Network

About the author: *The Free Expression Network is an alliance of organizations dedicated to protecting the First Amendment.*

Editor's note: The following viewpoint is a petition by the Free Expression Network entitled "An Appeal to Reason." It was written in mid-1999 in response to the "Appeal to Hollywood" petition that is also reprinted in this chapter. The Free Expression Network's petition has been signed by organizations such as the National Coalition Against Censorship and the National Campaign for Freedom of Expression. Individuals can sign the petition via the Internet at www.freeexpression.org.

Recently, a group of prominent Americans, including current and former public officials, issued a statement decrying violence in entertainment that they called an "Appeal to Hollywood." While there is certainly much to criticize in the media, this appeal is likely to do more harm than good. By promoting the idea that violent imagery causes crime and should be suppressed, it encourages government censorship.

We reject this approach and urge public officials and Hollywood executives to avoid simplistic responses and sound-bite solutions to complex social problems. There is no evidence that banning violence in the media will do anything to deter crime. Despite the claim in the Appeal to Hollywood that there is "overwhelming" evidence that entertainment violence has "harmful effects," a 1993 report by the National Research Council, a division of the National Academy of Sciences, did not even include exposure to media violence among the risk factors for violent behavior. In its 350 pages, the study, *Understanding and Preventing Violence,* devoted only four paragraphs to the question of whether the media cause violence, noting only that scientists do not agree. The purported link between media violence and crime is further undermined by the fact that the crime rate is now the lowest it has been in recent decades.

Media Violence Has Artistic Value

If censorship will not reduce crime, it will definitely prevent artists from exploring the subject of violence and frustrate efforts to understand a fundamental aspect of human behavior. Art imitates life, and violence has always been a part of life. Violence has been portrayed in art and entertainment throughout history, in both refined and popular fare: the Roman Circus and the wrestling match, public executions and the evening news, Shakespeare and Punch and Judy. The fact that audiences have always been fascinated by both real and simulated violence should come as no surprise. Art and entertainment are safe windows through which to view a world that is sometimes too terrible to contemplate otherwise. They allow us to examine our darkest fears. They also enable us to feel pity and even move us to attempt to fight the evils that they portray.

To appreciate the importance of violent imagery to artistic, intellectual and philosophical endeavors, consider the violence in the Bible, *The Iliad, Agamemnon,* Faulkner's *Light in August,* and James Dickey's *Deliverance;* in films such as *Paths of Glory, The Seventh Seal,* and *The Godfather;* in Picasso's *Guernica* and almost all religious art graphically depicting the Crucifixion; and in theater ranging from Shakespeare (*Macbeth, Henry V, Titus Andronicus*) to the Grand Guignol Theater's horror shows.

> *"Preventing our young from seeing the ugliness and brutality of violence deprives them of the knowledge they need to understand and resist it."*

The attack on violence in the media is the latest battle in a campaign for "decency" that has been going on for centuries and includes attacks on novels, comic books, and even Elvis Presley. It is worth remembering that Mozart's *Marriage of Figaro* was once considered "low class" entertainment, as were Shakespeare's comedies and other works we now see to contain great artistry and valuable commentary. *South Park* may never rise to such exalted heights, but it offers humor, fantasy, satire, and irreverence, all of which surely have redeeming value. While some believe that the exploration of dark fantasies in *The Basketball Diaries* actually led to a school shooting, others see it as a powerful antidote to anti-social behavior.

The Threat of Censorship

Although the rhetoric of the Appeal to Hollywood focuses on protecting children, it advocates a system of self-censorship by the entertainment industry that would also limit what adults could see by creating "minimum standards for violent, sexual and degrading material for each medium, below which producers can be expected not to go." This would threaten not only *South Park* but innovative adult programming like the HBO dramatic series, *The Sopranos.* Despite the claims in the Appeal to Hollywood that these codes would not create "wholesale strictures on artistic creativity," we should recall the impact of the infamous Hays Office, whose Production Code enforced "minimum standards" and prescribed exactly how movie directors could depict violence, sex, religion, and the flag.

We are told that self-censorship is acceptable because government has no role in enforcement. Yet it is clear that the goal of the Appeal is to chill certain forms of expression. Moreover, some signers of the Appeal have openly advocated government regulation if self-regulation doesn't work, and proposals currently in Congress make the threat of government censorship very real.

A Misguided Approach

Even if it were possible to censor only what children could see, the Appeal to Hollywood would be misguided. It suggests that violence is never an appropriate subject for children. Yet the word "children" includes kids from two to 17 and encompasses people of vastly different maturity levels. Certainly, most people agree that older minors should be able to see *Schindler's List* or *The Godfather.* Like *Boyz 'n the Hood,* these movies provide the perfect antidote for "escapist" entertainment by stripping violence of its glamour and emphasizing the value of human life. Preventing our young from seeing the ugliness and brutality of violence deprives them of the knowledge they need to understand and resist it.

No rating system can separate "good" violence from "bad." To some extent, that distinction is in the eye of the beholder. Even if "bad" violence could be precisely targeted, however, the ideas it represents and its power to influence behavior cannot be neutralized by suppressing offensive speech and images. To counter destructive ideas and behavior requires us to see them for what they are, and to speak out forcefully and effectively against them. The best response to hateful speech is still "more speech, not enforced silence."

The Appeal to Hollywood says that allowing children to have unsupervised access to media "is the moral equivalent of letting them go play on the freeway." We reject this hyperbolic claim as unreasonable, uninformed, and misguided. We should not blur the line between thoughts and action.

It is actions by people that kill and injure others, not their thoughts or fantasies. When we teach a child that he can blame his misbehavior on a TV show, film, song, video game, or Internet site that "made me do it," we undermine the idea that we are responsible for our own actions and open the way to more violence.

We join in the call to Hollywood executives to provide the highest quality entertainment possible. We also urge them to resist the pressure to create taboos, villainize art and artists, and constrain the creative imagination.

The Government Should Not Regulate the Marketing of Violent Media

by Virginia Postrel

About the author: *Virginia Postrel is the editor of* Reason *magazine and the author of* The Future and Its Enemies: The Growing Conflict Over Creativity, Enterprise, and Progress.

Showing the public relations savvy we expect from media moguls, the heads of the Hollywood studios declined to testify [in May of 1999] when the Senate Commerce Committee held hearings on "marketing violence to children." So when television reported the story, viewers saw movie clips of Keanu Reeves facing off against evil, rather than a tape of an anonymous executive squirming in the witness chair. Films remained works of art, protected by the First Amendment, rather than mere corporate products to be regulated at Washington's whim.

The distinction didn't last. At the hearings, Senator Joseph Lieberman, Democrat of Connecticut, hinted of things to come: "Joe Camel has, sadly, not gone away. He's gone into the entertainment business."

The Senator threatened the possibility of asking the Federal Trade Commission "to see if the entertainment industry is engaging in false advertising or unfair trade practices."

Before Congress could act, President Clinton delivered—much to the shock of his loyal supporters in Hollywood. He ordered an F.T.C. inquiry into "whether and how video game, motion picture and recording industries market to children violent and other material rated for adults." It will consider, for instance, whether these businesses advertise in media with large youth audiences and whether they adequately enforce existing, supposedly voluntary, rating systems.

The investigation will cost the taxpayers about $1 million. It will cost its targets millions more.

The F.T.C. probe is not just the usual telegenic show trial, good for a few headlines. The commission will exercise de facto subpoena power, demanding proprietary memos, private E-mail and internal marketing studies.

The inquiry will not end when the cameras go away. It will grind on, digging for dirt until it finds some. As Mr. Lieberman suggested, the model is the tobacco industry—the most demonized business in America.

This approach depends on defining movies not as stories or images but as products—which, of course, they are. It is the perfect campaign for an Administration working to restore the pre-Reagan punch of regulatory agencies.

By attacking free markets, the Clinton Administration can challenge free speech without abandoning its liberal image. "Many in the entertainment industry haven't grasped the distinction between marketing and creative license," an unnamed White House official told the *Los Angeles Times*.

Regulating creativity is bad; regulating marketing is O.K. The President is embracing virtue czar William Bennett's formulation that "this is predatory capitalism."

Just as Mr. Bennett's culture war means conservatives must break with free markets, so President Clinton's regulatory assault means liberals must abandon free speech. The probe looks like business regulation, but the real goal is content restriction.

> *"[Regulating the marketing of violent movies] punishes Hollywood for making products that powerful people think are immoral."*

After all, the inquiry makes little sense in the context of the F.T.C.'s mission. The agency is supposed to thwart "consumer injury," which suggests unhappy customers. But the tens of millions of people who bought tickets to *The Matrix* aren't complaining. The Liebermans, Bennetts and Clintons, who think moviegoers shouldn't have bought those tickets, are.

Yet movie advertisements aren't deceptive. Trailers for action movies show gunfire and explosions. Those for horror movies are scary. Nobody who saw an advertisement for *I Know What You Did Last Summer* expected a romantic comedy.

Supreme Court precedent allows the F.T.C. to regulate nondeceptive advertising as "unfair" only if it violates a public policy well established in law. But the movie rating system is voluntary. The First Amendment prohibits the sort of content restrictions that would inevitably come with a mandatory system.

The F.T.C. probe punishes Hollywood for making products that powerful people think are immoral. It sets a dangerous precedent for both free speech and consumer choice.

Culture warriors call movies they dislike "cultural pollution"—the toxic waste of greedy corporations. They scoff at the notion that such "pollution" is difficult to identify and assume their judgments are universally shared. "Can you not distinguish between *Casino* and *Macbeth,* or *Casino* and *Braveheart,* or

The Basketball Diaries and *Clear and Present Danger?*" Mr. Bennett rhetorically asked the Senate committee. "I can make that distinction." His eagerness is chilling.

Regulatory agencies don't let consumers make their own judgments about pollution. They simply ban it. The F.T.C. is not the Cultural Protection Agency, but involving it does change the terms of the debate. By treating moviegoers as victims of corporate malfeasance, rather than willing consumers of art, the Clinton Administration has taken a significant step toward transforming Keanu Reeves into Joe Camel.

Parents Should Teach Children to Critically Evaluate Violent Media Content

by Katey LaFrance

About the author: *Katey LaFrance is a contributing columnist to* Liberal Opinion Week.

Who could read or watch the news about the Springfield, Oregon, school shootings, without tears in their eyes; without utter dismay and outrage in their hearts; without feeling an urgent and intense demand for immediate disarmament of our nation, as the school's wrestling coach, Gary Bowden, has called for?

Guns are indiscriminate. They have no consciousness which cares whose lives they end. Guns are made to kill. That is the main reason they are manufactured: to take down that trophy buck, that killer wolf, or, in some peoples' minds: the enemy, meaning anyone who wrongs them.

Advocates of gun ownership often cite statistics of automobile deaths versus death from guns, absurdly asking if we would outlaw cars as well for the killings they cause. Cars are made for benign purposes. Automakers do not draw their blueprints with killing specifically in mind. In crash tests, their goal is not to see how many test dummies a car can mow down within seconds upon arrival at a school or on the freeway. Even in cases of road rage, a gun is still the preferred weapon of choice; a vehicle is only the incentive or means to use the gun.

What really causes one to recoil in disbelief and dismay is wondering what kind of nation we are when children view violence as the only means of resolution. We cannot blame it on television. We are told grandparents grew up with very violent folk stories which did not, apparently, incite them to kill. Television executives do not plan their programs to deliberately incite violence. Studies claim the Japanese release their rage through their violent television programs and video games, rather than each other, attesting to their lower crime rate.

Children's Viewing Habits Have Changed

The way America watches television has changed. The way we watch our children has changed. In the fifties and sixties, watching TV used to be a family affair; everyone would gather 'round to watch a favorite.

Even in the seventies, when my children were growing up, we, as parents, sat down with them to view what we considered to be good programming. We discussed and critiqued what they watched, making sure they didn't grow up thinking everything could be assuaged by gunfights, taking a pill, or colouring their hair a certain shade of blonde. They were restricted and monitored. They were allowed to watch adult programs, as long as there was interaction with us as to the truth and probability of content. Each of them has grown to become productive, peaceful sorts. None of them would choose a gun as a first, or even last, resort for problem-solving.

Today's children mostly watch TV on their own. If they come from the middle to upper classes they probably have a television in their room, while mom and dad each have their own to watch elsewhere in the house. Often, parents use television, willingly or unwillingly, as a baby-sitter or incentive to children; to quiet them down,

"[The v-chip] does not teach children the discernment which they will need as they become adults."

to entertain them. With the isolation of each to their corners, comes poor or little judgment of what they see happening in programs of all hours of the day. To restrict certain shows to what is supposedly bedtime for children is ridiculous. When one can tune into soaps and vile talk shows such as Jerry Springer, there is little left which need be censored to later hours.

Teach Critical Thinking and Nonviolence

We do not need to monitor the content of television as much as teach parents and other childcare givers the importance of limits and discussion about what is offered for daily viewing. Children's minds are like sponges; they soak up everything they see and hear without discernment for reality. They need guidance and discipline; to be taught critical thinking skills and non-violent means of resolving their differences or grievances.

The far right would have us believe Armageddon is at our doorstep. They, and other groups which share their so-called "family values," would have us believe our schools are failing when they teach children self-esteem; to feel good about themselves; to think for themselves; to learn to talk things out instead of resort to violence. They would also have us believe our country's problems are the result of our teachers, the government, the "new world order," the demise of

Hitler, the rise of liberalism in the sixties; in short, the fault of everyone else except the individual and themselves. Their paranoia and fear spills over into conventional society. Using scare tactics of volatile rhetoric, their sense of urgency spurs even the most non-violent persons to explore lethal ways of protection.

Each of us starts out in a nucleus of home. Some are better than others; most have some sort of conflict and/or dysfunctionality. Many of us rise above, overcome, and continue to progress, making it through our difficulties with the help of friends, family, and professionals.

Government Efforts Cannot Replace Good Parenting

Today's parents expect the government to protect their children from everything, including television. The v-chip came about because most parents are unwilling or unable to take the time to monitor what their children are doing, let alone what they watch on television. The irony is a v-chip is not critical; it does not teach children the discernment which they will need as they become adults. By not sitting down with them, by not commenting and discussing with them what they see on TV, at the movies, on the Internet, and in print, parents are abdicating their prime responsibility in raising their children. By not taking responsibility for the content of their daily lives, by not teaching them how to cope, parents have given up their position as the first line of defense against the insidious spread of violence which is portrayed in a society with such utter disregard for consequences.

While it is unrealistic to believe our country will ever totally disarm, even for the sake of the children, it is reasonable to expect parents to accept their responsibilities and rely on themselves in teaching their children the importance, tools, and skills of non-violent resolution.

Young People Should Not Be Barred from R-Rated Movies

by Rhys Southan

About the author: *Rhys Southan is associate entertainment editor for the* Daily Texan, *the student newspaper of the University of Texas.*

On the defensive from rabid legislators who want to capitalize on the Littleton shooting, the National Association of Theater Owners (NATO) announced [in June 1999] that it will rigorously enforce the R-ratings handed down by the Motion Picture Association of America (MPAA). Rather than decreasing violence, this discriminatory move, masked by false intentions of child protection, will only strengthen an outdated and inflexible ratings system that should be abolished.

In its current form, the rating board vaguely warns parents about "objectionable" content. Movies rated PG-13 or below are open to all, but an R-rating demands parental accompaniment, and NC-17 movies are off limits to all non-adults without exception.

According to MPAA founder Jack Valenti, "The basic mission of the rating system is a simple one: to offer to parents some advance information about movies so that parents can decide what movies they want their children to see or not to see." The MPAA's style of providing information is more stifling than helpful in the midst of the information revolution. An R-rating is too broad to take seriously, and the terms "violence, language, nudity, sensuality and drug abuse" alone leave a lot to the imagination.

Screen It! (www.screenit.com) is one superior resource. On this Web site, the potentially offensive content of all movies released is described in detail, answering every question a concerned parent or child might have. The main man behind the site, Jim Judy, is wise enough not to subscribe to the age suggestions of the ratings board. "No two children are alike," Judy explains. "For example,

Reprinted from "Making Movies Child-Proof," by Rhys Southan, *University Wire,* June 16, 1999. Reprinted with permission from the author.

111

one 9-year-old might be able to handle a certain type of scene, while another child of that same age can't. Or a given 10-year-old might be able to handle material that a 13-year-old can't. That's why any parental source that gives out ages is anything but accurate or even useful."

The MPAA's lie about only providing information is betrayed with its elitist NC-17 rating that doesn't even allow parents to make the decision. The real purpose of the MPAA is to stave off snip-happy politicians, but *censorship* is censorship, even if not directly governmental. The MPAA gets to play innocent by saying that filmmakers don't technically have to censor their film, but when it's between maintaining artistic integrity and losing a large segment of the audience, studios force filmmakers to trim for the desired rating.

This system generally hurts independent filmmakers who can't afford to make even small re-edits. Such movies are often R-rated for language alone, while studio backed movies like *Titanic,* with full frontal nudity and thousands of dead bodies, get off with PG-13 ratings because of their clout.

No 13-year-old is going to kill a bunch of people because he heard Hugh Grant say a naughty word in *Four Weddings and a Funeral.* Many of the best movies are R, and yet the young aren't allowed to see these examples of quality filmmaking without a parent tagging along, making them even more likely to rot their brains with idiotic Adam Sandler films. NATO claims to have turned away millions of dollars by enforcing ratings in the past, but a lot of that lost revenue is recovered by forcing parents to see R-rated movies their kids can't attend alone.

On the news there are horror stories about underage kids admitted to movies without IDs, but what about the true problem of teen-agers who aren't allowed to see some movies relevant to their lives? A six-year-old who tries to see *Tarzan* but accidentally stumbles into *Ravenous* may have nightmares, but a gay 15-year-old who wants to see a movie about the tribulations of closeted teens deserves to see *Get Real.* Even kids who are old enough

> *"[Enforcing R-ratings at movie theaters] will only strengthen an outdated and inflexible ratings system that should be abolished."*

may be denied admission because without a driver's license, most teenagers don't have identification. Some 17-year-olds don't drive, and many states are now implementing higher age minimums for getting licensed, leaving legal teens without IDs.

Everyone should know what they're in for before seeing a movie, but our institution-happy society is taking away everyone's rights by child-proofing the country. If the parents so paranoid about what their kids are exposed to would just do their jobs, the MPAA and other purveyors of age-based regulations would perish like so many campers in a *Friday the 13th* sequel.

Chapter 4

How Should the Problem of Media Violence Be Addressed?

Chapter Preface

On March 5, 1995, Sarah Edmundson and her boyfriend Ben Darrus, who had watched the 1994 movie *Natural Born Killers* repeatedly while on acid, went on a shooting spree, killing one person and injuring another at random stops along a stretch of Oklahoma highway. The two shooters were tried and convicted, but the family of Patsy Byers, one of the victims, also filed a civil lawsuit against the movie studio Warner Brothers and everyone associated with the making and distributing of the film, including its director Oliver Stone.

Stone's film graphically depicts the exploits of a boyfriend-and-girlfriend team of serial killers. Stone insists that he intended the film as a parody of the news media's fascination with violent crime; critics say the film itself glorifies serial killers. However one views the film, writes Susan J. Douglas in the *Nation*, "No recent movie has drawn more charges that it inspired real-life mayhem than Oliver Stone's *Natural Born Killers*."

The Byers's attorneys accuse Stone and Warner Brothers of "distributing a film which they knew or should have known would cause and inspire people to commit crimes." But, according to *Newsweek* writer Mark Miller, Stone enjoys considerable protection under the First Amendment's guarantee of free speech. The Byers family's lawyers must show that Stone intended to incite violence, and that the movie led to imminent lawlessness.

In a sense, the case bears some similarity to the so-called tobacco wars, which culminated in November 1998 when the nation's largest cigarette companies agreed to pay $208 billion to over forty states that had sued them in order to recoup the costs of treating people with lung cancer and other smoking-related illnesses. Just as the tobacco companies argued that smoking is a voluntary choice, producers of violent movies argue that they do not force people to commit violence. Nevertheless, the tobacco settlement set a major precedent for class-action lawsuits, and many people have wondered whether the manufacturers of other potentially harmful products—including, perhaps, violent media—should also be held accountable for the damage they may cause.

As of March 2000, the *Natural Born Killers* case is still before the courts. Its resolution could settle some questions about whether the producers of violent movies are responsible for the effects a film might have on viewers. The authors in the following chapter debate whether litigation against filmmakers is an appropriate response to the problem of media violence. They also explore other ways that individuals and society as a whole might address the issue.

The Entertainment Industry Should Be Held Liable for the Effects of Media Violence

by John P. McCarthy

About the author: *John P. McCarthy has written about television and film for* TV Guide, Daily Variety, Film Quarterly, *and the* British Journal of Aesthetics.

Contrary to press reports and spin by parties with vested interests, the summit on youth violence convened by President Clinton on May 10, 1999, was not a complete failure. It was the occasion for a breakthrough concerning the television industry. At that meeting the chairman of ABC, Bob Iger, reportedly said of his entertainment industry colleagues: "When the finger is pointed at them about violence, they say their media has no influence; but they turn around and say just the opposite to advertisers. We should all admit our media has an influence."

At long last someone with real power inside television has acknowledged a connection between what people watch and the violence they commit. And while Mr. Iger's comments were self-serving—since few of his peers showed up—I choose to read them as a small yet significant step toward better television. Consider it the equivalent of a tobacco company chief admitting his product is addictive and harmful to your health.

With an industry executive on record as admitting what everyone else has known all along—television has some deleterious effects—what can be done to mitigate the negative influences that may even have contributed to school shootings?

Even if it be granted that there is no cause and effect relationship between violence and watching television depictions of violence, the general coarsening of the culture reflected by television is reason enough to want to rein in television's excesses. Alongside moral considerations there are aesthetic values, issues of taste, that must be measured. But no one in Washington, let alone in Hollywood, is prepared to question the public's taste. There has been talk of legislation aimed at imposing limits on programming. I am loathe, however, to allow lawmakers to enter the First Amendment minefield under any circumstances, especially when emotions are running so high. Morality, as it has been often said, cannot be legislated. Neither can taste.

Anyone looking to the television-ratings system and the V-chip for remedies can only be disheartened. For any number of reasons, these devices have had little impact. Their biggest drawback is that they are tools the viewer must employ that do not alter the content of the programming itself.

A Difficult Question

That leads to a more specific question. What will persuade those who finance, make, distribute and sponsor programming to exercise self-restraint? Newton Minow, the former chairman of the Federal Communications Commission who once called television a "vast wasteland," has made a second career out of trying to shame the industry into mending its ways. In a *Washington Post* opinion piece on May 11, 1999, he urged the industry to return to the code of standards adopted by the National Association of Broadcasters in 1952. Asking programmers to come together and remember their duty to the public is not likely, however, to garner results. Adopting a voluntary code of conduct is impossible today, when so many new players (including all the cable channels) would have to come on board. Except for the occasional public service announcement, the broadcasters' obligation to safeguard the welfare of the viewing public is a distant memory. Besides, there are practical hurdles. Would such a code have teeth? How could it be enforced?

"The only way to clean up television is in court."

The truth is that only a compelling financial incentive will persuade the television industry to stop bombarding us with violent images. Advertising revenue is what makes most broadcast television possible (except for premium cable channels), but approaching the problem from that angle is not the answer. As Bob Iger observed, advertisers pay billions of dollars each year on the assumption that the shows they sponsor will be influential in the sense of attracting viewers. Right here is a crucial point that is often overlooked. The ads are often worse than the shows when it comes to violence, vulgarity and a general disrespect for vital human values. Even soap is peddled lasciviously. So advertisers are just as reluctant as programmers to support reform of content, because they would have to clean up their ads. Their bottom line would be at risk as well.

There is some good news from the advertising front, however. *TV Guide* reported on May 1, 1999, that a coalition of advertisers (no names were given) had initiated a plan to pay premium ad rates for shows that "don't flaunt sex, violence, or crude language." If this comes to pass, it would certainly turn the tables on programmers. They would be paid more money for making wholesome fare. I suspect that in practice such a scheme would be like preaching to the choir. Most of the extra money would go to outlets that are already offering such positive material. It is unlikely that other stations would switch to broadcasting unobjectionable shows simply because those programs would allow them to charge, say, 10 percent more for a 30-second spot hawking the next must-have toy or the best deal on life insurance for seniors. The financial impact of the plan would be minimal. It could improve the quality and quantity of programming that already has a positive influence, but the bad stuff would be left untouched.

> *"If programmers can, at least in theory, be held financially liable for the effects of what they make, then they might apply a little more thought to the product."*

The viewing public has few options when it comes to flexing its financial muscle. Boycotting the products of advertisers who sponsor objectionable programming only draws more attention both to the product and to the offensive material. The suggestion—almost as utopian as Minow's—that viewers simply not watch objectionable shows assumes, among other things, that the Nielsen rating system, which is used to determine the rates advertisers will be charged, accurately measures viewership. Millions of households would have to turn off their sets when a program became offensive, and those millions would have to include the majority of Nielsen households. (I've never known anyone from a Nielsen household.)

A grass-roots campaign against a show and its advertisers can put a dent in ratings and scare off sponsors. But that doesn't make a lasting impression on programmers. Most new shows are canceled anyway, and whether or not they will meet opposition down the line from irate viewers or squeamish advertisers doesn't enter into the equation. There's too much else to worry about, including making a new show salacious enough to capture the all-important 18 to 35 demographic.

Litigation: The Public's Only Recourse

No, the only way to clean up television is in court. Litigation, that all-American method for seeking redress, stands the best chance of changing the behavior of those who are responsible for obscenely violent television. Families of school shooting victims are already suing the makers of violent movies and video games. Lawsuits against the entertainment industry in the wake of the Columbine High School massacre are sure to follow.

I have misgivings, however, about civil suits like these. Chief among these doubts is uncertainty as to whether a causal connection can ever be proven. But that's the beauty of our legal system. This question can only be decided case by case. But if programmers can, at least in theory, be held financially liable for the effects of what they make, then they might apply a little more thought to the product. In this area a little more thought would be an exponential increase.

The Entertainment Industry Should Not Be Sued for Producing Violent Entertainment

by Jesse Walker

About the author: *Jesse Walker is an associate editor of* Reason *magazine.*

Rose Dyson wouldn't quite cop to being a censor. She had bragged about how her group, Canadians Concerned About Violence in Entertainment, had helped keep Howard Stern off the air in part of her country; she had endorsed the V-chip, though she felt it would be "only 10 percent of the solution"; she wanted to sue filmmakers whose movies may have prompted copycat crimes. She even admitted to supporting the old "Suicide Solution" case from the '80s, in which a father took Ozzy Osbourne to court over the song he was convinced had driven his son to kill himself.

But the word censor has negative connotations, and whenever I told Dyson that she sounded like one to me, she'd say, "I think we need to redefine censorship." She never offered an alternative definition.

We were sitting in a bar in Athens, Ohio, where we were both attending a conference of media critics. I was there because I wanted the media to be more open. She was there because she wanted them to be more peaceful.

Video violence, she told me, was a "cheap industrial pollutant," and she didn't mean that metaphorically. The companies that "manufacture" violent movies, she explained, should be as responsible for their products' effects as a factory that spits real poisons into the air or water. Nor did it matter what the film-makers' intentions were: While she didn't buy the argument that *Natural Born Killers* was an invective against media violence (implying that she either hadn't seen the movie or wasn't very bright), it wouldn't matter to her if it was. "Artistic merit," she said, "should not be a defense."

That was the one point where we agreed, since I figure the First Amendment protects bad art as well as good.

The *Natural Born Killers* Lawsuit

I had brought up *Natural Born Killers* because it is the target of an increasingly notorious lawsuit. [In 1995] in Louisiana, 19-year-old Sarah Edmondson shot and paralyzed a convenience store clerk, Patsy Byers, as part of a multistate crime spree. Byers' husband responded by suing Time Warner for releasing the film and Oliver Stone for directing it, arguing that the movie had incited the crime. (Edmondson and her boyfriend say they watched it more than 20 times before they started their spree.) Despite the case's obvious First Amendment problems, the trial judge agreed to hear it, citing a similar suit against Paladin Press as a precedent. Now the Stone case itself is a precedent: With it moving forward, no one has stopped a similar suit blaming the film *The Basketball Diaries*—along with several other cultural artifacts, including some violent video games and two nudie Web sites—for the shooting deaths of three girls in Kentucky.

> *"The First Amendment protects bad art as well as good."*

The lawsuits have been endorsed by the usual alliance of social conservatives and liberal social engineers, the same combination that's made war on cinematic speech since the New Dealers and the National Legion of Decency united behind the Hays Office and its infamous Production Code. But this is uncharted territory. As bad as the old censorship was, it did not require artists and entertainers to measure in advance every possible effect their work could have on every possible person in their audience.

Slowly, a debate about art has degenerated into a debate about externalities. And that's very dangerous indeed. After all, culture consists of nothing but spillover effects.

The threshold for censorship used to be "redeeming social merit": Any positive effect was, in theory, enough to let a book be. The Dyson standard turns this on its head: It says any negative effect is sufficient to snuff something out.

Art Is Ambiguous

In other words, it outlaws art itself. From *Hamlet* to *Huck Finn* to *Happiness,* most great works of art (and a lot of lesser efforts) are ambiguous, or at least open-ended; they invite debate, demanding different responses from the audience. Any really interesting movie about violence is going to leave some issues open, if only because so many of the questions it will pose will not lend themselves to pat answers. Some find this insightful; for the Dyson crowd, it's inciteful.

Is *True Lies* a mindless action movie, a parody of mindless action movies, or a corrosive satire of the American family? Is *Fargo* a satire of bourgeois virtues or a defense of them? In the *Godfather* trilogy, is the Mafia admirable or repulsive? In each case the answer is "all of the above," by the filmmakers' deliberate design.

And even if only one answer is correct—even if the director has a pat point to make—what then? *Natural Born Killers* is obviously opposed to violence, yet it nonetheless may have inspired some violent behavior. Nasty Nazi movies like *The Eternal Jew* were made to foment anti-Semitism, but they're sometimes shown today to fan fears of bigotry.

You never know to what uses your work will one day be put: When the good folks at CBS created *The Bob Newhart Show,* they never dreamed they were also inventing a drinking game. (How many people have been killed by drivers inebriated by a round of "Hi, Bob"? Should their families be allowed to sue Newhart?)

Some audiences impose weird new meanings onto books and movies, drawing them into elaborate personal mythologies. In *Crumb,* Terry Zwigoff's documentary about the cartoonist R. Crumb and his family, one of the artist's brothers discusses the weird, vaguely sexual fantasies he projected onto Byron Haskin's film of *Treasure Island* as a boy, filling notebooks with his take on the story and bullying his siblings into re-enacting key scenes.

No one at Disney could have imagined that their movie would have inspired such a reaction, any more than the makers of *Star Trek* could have foreseen that their series would inspire a new genre of fan pornography, centered on the potential liaisons between Spock and Kirk. [In 1997], a crank book called *The Bible Code* became a best-seller because it allowed readers a new way to engage in the ancient art of finding whatever meanings they pleased in the Bible. God, presumably, is turning in his Nietzschean grave.

> *"The* **Natural Born Killers** *and* **Basketball Diaries** *lawsuits . . . [have a] chilling effect on free speech."*

There are plenty of good reasons to be against the *Natural Born Killers* and *Basketball Diaries* lawsuits, from their chilling effect on free speech to their willingness to let criminals disavow responsibility for their acts. But the suits are wrong on their own terms, too. Sure, art can be an influence for ill, just as it can do good. Courts do not award extra dollars to entertainers for the unforeseen positive byproducts of their work. Why penalize them for the less fortunate consequences of what they do?

Individuals Should Address the Problem of Media Violence by Making Better Entertainment Choices

by Anne P. Dupre

About the author: *Anne P. Dupre is a professor at the University of Georgia School of Law and a former law clerk for Supreme Court Justice Harry A. Blackmun.*

I am not a psychic, but I am going to make a prediction, though I hope I am wrong. I predict that, if and when the film "American Psycho" is released, the police will deal with at least one killing which copies the murders and mutilations in the movie. The prospective picture is based on a novel by Bret Easton Ellis, and its makers attempted to sign Leonardo DiCaprio to the lead role. [Editor's note: The film was released in April 2000.]

The book depicts a Wall Street Yuppie who tortures and kills for the fun of it. He murders 18 people, including a child that he kills at the zoo. He reserves his most sadistic torture for women. In one scene in the book, the killer attaches jump leads to a female victim's nipples. In another, he has sex with the head of a woman he has decapitated. Some favorite weapons he uses on women are a nail gun, power drill, chain saw, and, if you can imagine (or want to), a hungry rat. Get ready, America, and pray that this movie does not light a fuse in someone living near you.

You may question why—if I can make a prediction that someone will die—the law has no mechanism to prevent this potential harm. It is no secret that some people like to copy killings they see in movies. Films give people a sense of what depravity is possible and a movie star to model after. Copycat killings are alleged to have been linked to such pictures as "Natural Born Killers," "Warlock," "The Money Train," "The Basketball Diaries," and "Child's Play 3," among others. It is true that people also can read about psychotic killers in books, but words on the page do not seem to inspire the same kind of frenzy blood on the screen can. Psychotic killers generally are not bookworms. Moreover, films reach a wider audience than most books.

Outlawing Media Violence Is Not Feasible

The first response to my prediction undoubtedly will be a shake of the head and an explanation that this is the price we have to pay for freedom of speech under the First Amendment. Anything else would be censorship. After all, the highly acclaimed "Saving Private Ryan" is graphically violent. Nightly news shows report violent acts every evening. In fact, the same day Kip Kinkel was arrested after shooting a number of schoolmates in Oregon, three boys in Missouri were foiled in an attempt to imitate the massacre in Jonesboro, Arkansas, wherein two boys shot fellow students from a nearby hillside after pulling the school fire alarm. (It is telling that those boy killers have been described as dressing like Rambo or looking like a Clint Eastwood or Arnold Schwarzenegger film character.)

We certainly should not ask that every potentially dangerous scene be deleted from every movie. "Saving Private Ryan" showed viewers how ordinary men could gain nobility in the midst of violence and bloodshed. Nor should we ask networks to cease reporting important news stories. Reporting on a school massacre helps the audience to analyze a serious national problem of juvenile violent crime and realize the sad truth that some young boys believe it is cool to be viewed as psychotic.

Nonetheless, a film like "American Psycho," if it is as vivid as the book, undoubtedly will test some people's views on the limits of First Amendment protection. In fact, First Amendment speech protection is not absolute. After all, we have seen how cigarette advertisements can be curtailed. One constitutional axiom was set forth by Justice Oliver Wendell Holmes when he stated that a person falsely yelling fire in a crowded theater is not protected by the First Amendment. The notion is that, if you say something when you know it is likely that people will be hurt reacting to your speech—the Supreme Court used the words "clear and present danger"—those words may not be protected. I predict that some alienated person (or persons)—impulsive, self-destructive, and full of rage—will see "American Psycho" and believe that, through its teachings, he can become Master of the Universe for a time. If I know it, so do the filmmakers. Indeed, these kinds of movies may be particularly enticing to people who feel powerless and on the margins of society. Through such pictures, they learn that,

> *"Even if one film may not inspire direct violent action in most children who see that movie, the effect is insidious as it creeps into the lexicon and corrupts American culture."*

if they do something that is utterly depraved, they may get at least some recognition, some attention, that will make up for whatever else is missing in their lives.

To be sure, millions of those who see the picture will harm no one as a result. They merely will watch the chronicle of a psychotic killer and go home, perhaps to view yet another set of grisly murders depicted on television. It also is true that, as the National Rifle Association proclaims, guns don't kill people; people kill people. Yet, many argue—in spite of the Second Amendment's protection of the right to bear arms—that certain kinds of guns should be outlawed because they may get into the hands of the wrong people. Moreover, most individuals who drive after consuming an excess of alcohol or break the speed limit do not harm others either, but there are laws that regulate and punish such conduct—laws that many want to make even stricter.

> *"If the First Amendment protects movies that may incite violence, there is no constitutional protection against empty theaters."*

It is a given that children will see this movie, despite any warning which may accompany it. After all, if parents like Kip Kinkel's give in to a youngster's demands for a gun, surely viewing a motion picture is not off-limits. Children, of course—as well as many adults—are unlikely to see the satire or the nihilistic vision in a movie. They merely see the glorification of barbarism. Even if one film may not inspire direct violent action in most children who see that movie, the effect is insidious as it creeps into the lexicon and corrupts American culture.

One does not need to advocate censorship to understand the harm that occurs. Sissela Bok, author of *Mayhem: Violence as Public Entertainment,* states that media violence undermines resilience and self-control. At the very least, those who see these pictures, especially children, undoubtedly must start to view deviancy in a different light over time. Kids and adults who watch the jumper clips, chain saws, power drills, and the rat will add such scenes to the mixture with the hundreds of other violent acts they have watched over the years, reinforced by whatever gore next month's movies and television shows will bring to them. It is easy to end up eventually with a different perspective on where the line for aberrant behavior begins. Senator Daniel Patrick Moynihan called this defining deviancy down, and the nation is in a terrifying spiral.

Saying "No" to Violent Movies

If the First Amendment protects movies that may incite violence, there is no constitutional protection against empty theaters. Indeed, director Stanley Kubrick voluntarily banned his film, "A Clockwork Orange," from being shown in Britain after some youths raped a young woman while performing "Singin' in the Rain," an act they had imitated from the movie. Simon & Schuster regarded the sexual violence in the book *American Psycho* as so nauseating that it canceled the original publication contract, sacrificing $300,000. (The book later was published elsewhere.) Surely it is possible for many gifted filmmakers to create a discerning and penetrating motion picture without indulging in the simplistic stimulation of graphic violence. Even without filmmakers volunteering to halt the deviancy spiral, economics surely would. If these movies were not profitable, they would not be made. Why do they draw enough people into the theater and video stores to be profitable?

The real reason why the film "American Psycho"—if and when it is made—will be just one more entry in the line of depravity is because the public is entertained. As viewers, we are, ironically, much like the main character in the book. The titillation both arouses and gratifies us. We feast on each shocking scene after the next. Some may try to hide their self-indulgence under the cloak of movie-speak: "Yes, it was extremely violent. But it had sharp dialogue, dark humor, great production values, and one could detect the auteur's vision." The truth is that we have been seduced and are unable or unwilling to cease luxuriating in this style to which we have become accustomed. For some, this may be due in part to the fact that most of us, in the affluent and sanitized world of the late 20th century, seldom are exposed to the gritty sights and smells that were a part of daily life in the 19th century.

We may be enticed by violence on film because we are so afraid of it in life. We can sit in a theater, enjoy the violent scene on the screen from a distance, and then go home—we hope—to safety. So we contribute to a perverse circularity whereby our habits actually may help to increase the violence we fear. Just as with other indulgences from which it is difficult to break free, we eventually need more potent doses of violence to titillate and shock. If the lurid rape scene in "The Accused" shocked us one year, we need Hannibal Lecter's cannibalism in "The Silence of the Lambs" the next. When cannibalism becomes de rigueur, it is time to bring on the rats.

The law will not come in and save us this time. Although we may use the law in various ways to protect us from the harm caused by cigarettes, it will not help us here. Violent and depraved films are protected by the First Amendment. Those trying to convince courts to recognize a civil action for damages against motion picture producers have been unsuccessful. This time, the buck stops with you.

> *"We contribute to a perverse circularity whereby our habits actually may help to increase the violence we fear."*

Think about that as you make your movie and television choices. Think about what it is in the collective American psyche that makes gruesome violence so alluring in film after film. Think about my prediction the next time you read how a rapist or killer has imitated the brutality depicted in the theater or on television. Then, you may want to make your own prediction about the future. You will not like what you see.

Teaching Media Literacy Can Help Address the Problem of Media Violence

by Pat Kipping

About the author: *Pat Kipping is president of the Association for Media Literacy–Nova Scotia.*

When my children were young, in a well-meaning effort to protect them from the horrors of TV and play violence, I became, like many good parents and peace activists, an unwitting participant in what Elizabeth Thoman at the Centre for Media Literacy in Los Angeles calls "the circle of blame." This is how it works. Viewers blame the producers for making violent programs. Producers blame the broadcasters for wanting programs that get high ratings. Broadcasters blame the advertisers for sponsoring highly rated programs regardless of content. Advertisers blame the viewers for watching and pushing up the ratings of violent shows. "We're only giving them what they want," they say. Everyone blames the government.

For 40 years, concerned parents, peace activists, and others have been indulging in this blaming exercise. It hasn't achieved anything. In fact, the amount of violent images and toys that children can see has increased dramatically over the past 40 years.

While we, and everyone else in this circle of blame, point self-righteous, accusing fingers at one another, waiting for someone else to do something, millions of children are sitting, while you read this article, in front of a TV or computer screen being thrilled, confused, or terrified by the violence they are seeing. It will have lasting effects. If we are genuinely concerned about today's children, then we must break this circle of blame and do something now.

Media literacy is a strategy which can be implemented immediately to change the way children are affected by violent television. In the long run, I

Reprinted from "Media Literacy: An Important Strategy for Building Peace," by Pat Kipping, *Peace Magazine*, January/February 1996. Reprinted with permission.

am certain that a comprehensive campaign of critical media literacy education will result in better television. I hope that eventually, a critical mass of media literate viewers will prove those advertisers wrong and drive down ratings for cheap, gratuitous violence. I know many producers would jump at the chance to make creative, pro-social, intelligent entertainment for children and adults. But in the short term, in the current climate of deregulation and self-regulation where corporate market values rule, I believe that media literacy is the *only* way to effectively deal with television violence.

In order to understand how media literacy can accomplish this, it is necessary to shift our thinking about the media away from the idea that it is a problem that can be solved or a system that can be resisted and accept that television, indeed all mass media, are here to stay. They have become an environment that must be navigated.

Remember what Marshall McLuhan said in his famous book, *The Medium is the Message:* "Any understanding of social and cultural change is impossible without a knowledge of the way the media work as environments." Media literacy is a well-developed tool we can use today to help our children understand and

> *"[Media literate people] know how to act. They are not acted on. In that way, media literate people are better citizens."*

learn to navigate this treacherous environment. Parents and educators can use its strategies to teach children and other viewers how to "read between the lines" of television.

Media literate people understand that:
- television is constructed to convey ideas, information, and news from someone else's perspective.
- specific techniques are used to create emotional effects. They can identify those techniques and their intended and actual effects.
- all media benefit some people and leave others out. They can pose and sometimes answer questions about who are the beneficiaries, who is left out and why.

Media literate people:
- seek alternative sources of information and entertainment.
- use television for their own advantage and enjoyment.
- are not used by television for someone else's advantage.
- know how to act. They are not acted on. In that way, media literate people are better citizens.

An Important Resource for Children

That's what I really want for my children and all the other children who will be adults sooner than the Canadian Radio-Television and Telecommunications Commission (CRTC) can say "let's consult on this some more . . .". I want them to have the resources to act for change in a world that increasingly allows too many children to experience the violence of poverty, abuse, and neglect.

Ursula Franklin once said, "Violence is resourcelessness." Critical media literacy is an important resource we must develop in our children. It would be a form of violence to deny them this resource while we wait for something better to come along.

Communities Should Have More Control over the Content of Mass Media

by George Gerbner

About the author: *Most famous for his research on television violence and "Mean World Syndrome," George Gerbner is founder and president of the Cultural Environment Movement and the author of numerous books on the media, including* The Future of Media: Digital Democracy or More Corporate Control?

Most of what we know, or think we know, we have never personally experienced. We live in a world erected by stories. Stories socialize us into roles of gender, age, class, vocation, and lifestyle, and offer models of conformity or targets for rebellion. They weave the seamless web of our cultural environment. Our stories used to be hand crafted, home made, community inspired. Now they are mostly mass produced and policy driven, the result of a complex manufacturing and marketing process we know as the mass media. This situation calls for a new diagnosis and a new prescription.

Three Types of Stories

The stories that animate our cultural environment have three distinct but related functions: to reveal how things work, to describe what things are, and to tell us what to do about them.

Stories of the first kind, revealing how things work, illuminate the all-important but invisible relationships and hidden dynamics of life. Fairy tales, novels, plays, comics, cartoons, and other forms of creative imagination and imagery are the basic building blocks of human understanding. They show complex causality by presenting imaginary action in total situations, coming to some conclusion that has a moral purpose and a social function. You don't have to believe the "facts" of Little Red Riding Hood to grasp the notion that big bad "wolves" victimize old women and trick little girls—a lesson in gender roles,

Reprinted from "The Stories We Tell," by George Gerbner, *Peace Review,* August/September 1999. Reprinted with permission from Taylor & Francis, Ltd., PO Box 25, Abingdon, Oxfordshire, OX14 3UE, UK.

fear, and power. Stories of the first kind build, from infancy on, the fantasy we call reality. I do not suggest that the revelations are false, which they may or may not be, but that they are synthetic, selective, often mythical, and always socially constructed.

Stories of the second kind depict what things are. These are descriptions, depictions, expositions, and reports abstracted from total situations. They fill in with "facts" the fantasies conjured up by stories of the first kind. They are the presumably factual accounts, the chronicles of the past and the news of today. Stories of what things are may confirm or deny some conception of how things work. Their high "facticity" (correspondence to actual events presumed to exist independently of the story) gives them special status in political theory and often in law. They give emphasis and credibility to selected parts of society's fantasies of reality. They convey information about finance, weddings, crime, lotteries, terrorists, and so on. They alert us to certain interests, threats, opportunities, and challenges.

> *"With the coming of the electronic age, that cultural environment is increasingly monopolized, homogenized, and globalized."*

Stories of the third kind tell us what to do. These are stories of value and choice. They present things, behaviors, or styles of life as desirable or undesirable, propose ways to obtain or avoid them, and the price to be paid for attainment or failure. They are the instructions, laws, regulations, cautionary tales, commands, slogans, sermons, and exhortations. Today most of them are called commercials.

Stories of the third kind clinch the lessons of the first two and turn them into action. They typically present an objective to be sought or to be avoided, and offer a product, service, candidate, institution, or action purported to help attain or avoid it. The lessons of fictitious Little Red Riding Hoods and their more realistic sequels prominent in everyday news and entertainment not only teach lessons of vulnerability, mistrust, and dependence but also help sell burglar alarms, more jails, and executions, all in the name of enhanced security.

Ideally, the three kinds of stories check and balance each other. But in a commercially driven culture, stories of the third kind pay for most of the first two. This creates a coherent cultural environment whose overall function is to provide a hospitable and effective context for stories that sell. With the coming of the electronic age, that cultural environment is increasingly monopolized, homogenized, and globalized. We must then look at the historic course of our journey to see what this new age means for us and for our children.

The Rise of Literacy

For the longest time in human history, stories were told only face-to-face. A community was defined by the rituals, mythologies, and imageries held in common. All useful knowledge was encapsulated in aphorisms and legends, proverbs and tales, incantations and ceremonies. Writing was rare and holy. Laboriously inscribed manuscripts conferred sacred power to their interpreters, the priests and ministers. State and church ruled in a symbiotic relationship of mutual dependence and tension. The state, composed of feudal nobles, was the economic, military, and political order; the church its cultural arm.

The industrial revolution changed all that. One of the first machines stamping out standardized artifacts was the printing press. Its product, the book, was a prerequisite for all the other upheavals to come. Printing began the industrialization of storytelling, and was arguably the most profound transformation in the humanization process.

The book could be given to all who could read, requiring education and creating a new literate class of people. Readers could now interpret the book (at first the Bible) for themselves, breaking the monopoly of priestly interpreters and ushering in the Reformation.

When the printing press was hooked up to the steam engine the industrialization of storytelling shifted into high gear. Rapid publication and mass transport created a new form of consciousness: modern mass publics. Publics are those loose aggregations of people who share some common consciousness of how things work, what things are, and what ought to be done—but never meet face-to-face. That was never before possible.

> *"For the first time in human history, children are born into homes where mass-produced stories reach them on the average more than seven hours a day."*

Stories could now be sent—often smuggled—across hitherto impenetrable or closely guarded boundaries of time, space, and status. The book lifts people from their traditional moorings as the industrial revolution uproots them from their local communities and cultures. They can now get off the land and go to work in far-away ports, factories, and continents, and have with them a packet of common consciousness—the book or journal—wherever they go.

The Telecommunications Era

The second great transformation, the electronic revolution, ushered in the telecommunications era. Its main medium, television, superimposes upon and reorganizes print-based culture. Unlike the industrial revolution, the new upheaval does not uproot people from their homes but transports them in their homes. It re-tribalizes modern society. It challenges and changes the role of both church and education in the new culture.

For the first time in human history, children are born into homes where mass-produced stories reach them on the average more than seven hours a day. Most waking hours, and often dreams, are filled with these stories. The stories do not come from families, schools, churches, neighborhoods, and often not even from their native countries. They come from a small group of distant conglomerates with something to sell.

The cultural environment in which we live has become the byproduct of marketing. The historic nexus of state and church is replaced by the new symbiotic relationship of state and television. The "state" itself is the twin institution of elected public government and selected private corporate government, ruling in the legal, military, and economic domains. Media, its cultural arm, are dominated

> *"Formula-driven assembly-line produced programs increasingly dominate the airways. . . . A central formula in this globalized system is that of violence."*

by the private establishment, despite their use of the public airways. Giant industries discharge their messages into the mainstream of common consciousness. Channels proliferate and new technologies pervade home and office while mergers and bottom-line pressures shrink creative alternatives and reduce diversity of content.

These changes may appear to be broadening local, parochial horizons, but they also mean a homogenization of outlooks and a limitation of alternatives. For media professionals, the changes mean fewer opportunities and greater compulsions to present life in saleable packages. Creative artists, scientists, humanists can still explore and enlighten and occasionally even challenge, but increasingly their stories must fit marketing strategies and priorities.

As audiences we pay dearly for our "free" news and entertainment through a surcharge added to the price of every advertised product. Allowing advertising costs to be a tax-deductible business expense is a further give-away of public money for private purposes.

Formula-Driven Media Violence

Broadcasting is the most concentrated, homogenized, and globalized medium. The top 100 U.S. advertisers pay for two-thirds of all network television. Four networks, allied to giant transnational corporations—our private Ministry of Culture—control the bulk of production and distribution, and shape the cultural mainstream. Other interests—religious, political or educational—lose ground with every merger.

Formula-driven assembly-line produced programs increasingly dominate the airways. The formulas themselves reflect the structure of power that produces them and function to preserve and enhance that structure of power. A central formula in this globalized system is that of violence. The pervasiveness of violent programming is a good example of how the media system works. It is also an indication of the magnitude and nature of the challenge before us.

Humankind may have had more bloodthirsty eras, but none as filled with images of crime and violence as the present. Overall, U.S. television networks doubled the time given to crime coverage between 1992 and 1993. News of crime surges to new highs, while violent crime rates remain essentially flat or decline. The overrepresentation of violence is especially clear in local television news. A 1994 University of Miami study of local television news, for example, found that time devoted to crime ranged from 23% to 50% of news time (averaging 32%) while violent crime in the city remained constant, involving less than 0.1% of the population.

Not only is it the case that local news shows are dominated by vivid images of violence, but in a high percentage of cases African-Americans and Latinos are shown as the perpetrators of that violence, contributing to a sense of fear and distrust, according to a 1994 study by Robert Entman for the Chicago Council on Urban Affairs. Another 1994 study by Johnstone, Hawkins and Michener looked at homicide news reporting and found that only one of three actual homicides was reported, and that the most likely to be selected were those in which the victims were white rather than black or Latino, contrary to the actual crime statistics.

Our own Cultural Indicators study of local news on Philadelphia television found that crime and/or violence items usually lead the newscast. Furthermore, 80% of crime and violence reported on Philadelphia local news was not even local to the city. It is as if a quota were imposed on the editorial staff which they have to fill from wherever they can.

"Happy Violence"

Violence is also prevalent in entertainment. The percentage of primetime television dramatic programs with overt physical violence was 58% in 1974, 73% in 1984, and 75% in 1994. The saturation of violent scenes was five per hour in 1974, five per hour in 1984, and five per hour in 1994—unchanged. In Saturday morning children's programs, scenes of violence occur between 20 and 25 times per hour. They are sugar coated with humor, to be sure, to make the pill of power easier to swallow.

Action movies cash in on this trend, increasing the violence level as each sequel comes out. Vincent Canby tells us the following in his *New York Times* article entitled "Body Count," published in July 1990. *Robocop*'s first rampage for law and order killed 32 people; *Robocop 2* slaughtered 81. The movie *Death Wish* claimed nine victims; in the sequel, the bleeding-heart-liberal-turned-vigilante disposed of 52 victims. Similarly *Rambo: First Blood* rambled through Southeast Asia leaving 62 corpses, while *Rambo III* visited Afghanistan killing 106.

> *"'Happy violence' is cool, swift, and painless, and always leads to a happy ending."*

Violence is a demonstration of power. Its principal lesson is to show quickly and dramatically who can get away with what against whom. It defines majority might and minority risk. It shows one's place in the societal pecking order.

This kind of story has consequences. Our surveys show that heavy viewers of television express a greater sense of apprehension and vulnerability than do light viewers in the same groups. Heavy viewers are also more likely than comparable groups of light viewers to overestimate their chances of involvement in violence; to believe that their neighborhoods are unsafe; to state that fear of crime is a very serious personal problem; and to assume that crime is rising, regardless of the facts of the case. Heavy viewers of television are also more likely to buy new locks, watchdogs, and guns "for protection" (thus becoming the major cause of handgun violence).

> *"There is no evidence that, cost and other factors being equal, violence per se gives audiences 'what they want.'"*

Moreover, viewers who see members of their own group underrepresented but overvictimized develop an even greater sense of apprehension and mistrust. Insecure, angry, mistrustful people may be prone to violence but are even more likely to be dependent on authority and susceptible to deceptively simple, strong, hard-line postures and appeals.

Violence is, of course, a legitimate, even necessary, news and dramatic feature to demonstrate the tragic costs of deadly compulsions. However, such a tragic sense of violence has been swamped by "happy violence" produced on the television dramatic assembly-line. "Happy violence" is cool, swift, and painless, and always leads to a happy ending. It occurs five times per hour, designed to deliver the audience to the next commercial in a receptive mood.

Media Violence Is Not a Result of Public Choice

What drives this media violence? The usual rationalization is that media violence "gives the public what it wants." This is disingenuous. The public rarely gets a fair choice of programming in which all elements but violence are equal. But besides this, there is no evidence that, cost and other factors being equal, violence per se gives audiences "what they want." As the trade paper *Broadcasting & Cable* said in an editorial on September 20, 1993, "the most popular programming is hardly violent as anyone with a passing knowledge of Nielsen ratings will tell you."

Our own study confirms this. We compared the ratings of over 100 violent and 100 non-violent shows aired at the same time on network television. The average Nielsen rating of the violent sample was 11.1; the rating for the non-violent sample was 13.8. The share of viewing households in the violent and non-violent samples, respectively, was 18.9 and 22.5. The non-violent sample was more highly rated than the violent sample for each of the five seasons studied. The amount and consistency of violence further increased the unpopularity gap.

Media violence is, in fact, a consequence of media economics. Concentration of ownership in media denies access to new entries and to alternative perspectives. Having fewer buyers for their products forces the remaining "content providers" deeper into deficit financing. As a consequence, most television and movie producers cannot break even on the U.S. domestic market. They are forced into video and foreign sales to make a profit. Therefore, they need a dramatic ingredient that requires no translation and fits any culture. That ingredient is violence.

Syndicators demand "action" (the code word for violence) because it travels well. As the producer of *Die Hard 2* said in the May 17, 1992, *New Yorker,* "Everyone understands an action movie. If I tell a joke, you may not get it, but if a bullet goes through the window, we all know how to hit the floor, no matter the language."

Violence dominates U.S. exports. We compared 250 U.S. programs exported to ten countries with 111 programs shown in the U.S. during the same year. Violence was the main theme of 40% of home-shown and 49% of exported programs. Crime/action series comprised 17% of home-shown and 46% of exported programs. NAFTA and GATT will dump even more mayhem on the world in the name of "free trade."

People suffer the media violence inflicted on them with diminishing tolerance. In a *Times-Mirror* national poll in 1993, for example, 80% said entertainment violence was "harmful" to society, compared with 64% in 1983.

> *"There is a liberating alternative. . . . It involves the development of an independent citizen voice in cultural policy making."*

Local broadcasters, legally responsible for what goes on the air, also oppose the overkill and complain about loss of control. *Electronic Media* reported on August 2, 1993, that in its own survey of 100 general managers, three out of four said there is too much needless violence on television and 57% would like to have "more input on program content decisions." A *U.S. News & World Report* survey published on April 30, 1994, found that 59% of media workers saw entertainment violence as a serious problem.

The Cultural Environment Movement

There is a liberating alternative. There is something we can do. It exists in various forms in all democratic countries. It involves the development of an independent citizen voice in cultural policy making. The Cultural Environment Movement (CEM) was launched for this purpose. Its Founding Convention was held in St. Louis, Missouri, in March 1996. It was the most diverse international assembly of leaders and activists in the field of culture and communication that has ever met. The 261 participants debated and approved a "People's Communication Charter," the "Viewer's Declaration of Independence," and developed recommendations for action from 15 task forces.

The concepts that motivated us were developed after 30 years of media research. It became clear that research is not enough; we must reclaim the rights gained through centuries of struggle. Working separately on individual issues, rallying to meet each individual crisis, was not sufficient. Treating symptoms instead of the wholesale manufacturing of the conditions that led to those symptoms was self-defeating. The new approach of the CEM seeks to treat the cause in a number of ways.

> *"[The Cultural Environment Movement] is working to build a new coalition . . . committed to broadening the freedom and diversity of communication."*

CEM is working to build a new coalition involving: media councils worldwide; teachers, students, and parents; groups concerned with children, youth, and aging; women's groups; religious and minority organizations; educational, health, environmental, legal, and other professional associations; consumer groups and agencies; associations of creative workers in the media and in the arts and sciences; independent computer network organizers and other organizations and individuals committed to broadening the freedom and diversity of communication.

CEM, and the coalition as a whole, opposes domination and works to abolish existing concentration of ownership and censorship (both of and by media), public or private. This involves extending rights, facilities, and influence to interests and perspectives other than the most powerful and profitable. It means involving in cultural decision making the less affluent and more vulnerable groups, including the marginalized, neglected, abused, exploited, physically or mentally disabled, young and old, women, minorities, poor people, recent immigrants—all those most in need of a decent role and a voice in a freer cultural environment.

There is also an international dimension, seeking out and cooperating with the cultural liberation forces of all countries that are working for the integrity and independence of their own decision making and against cultural domination and invasion. It is important to learn from countries that have already opened their media to the democratic process, and to help local movements, including in the most dependent and vulnerable countries of Latin America, Asia, and Africa (and also in Eastern Europe and the former Soviet republics), to invest in their own cultural development and to oppose aggressive foreign ownership and coercive trade policies that make such development more difficult.

Putting Culture on the Social-Political Agenda

Another weave of the work is supporting journalists, artists, writers, actors, directors, and other creative workers struggling for freedom from having to present life as a commodity designed for a market of consumers. By working with guilds, caucuses, labor, and other groups for diversity in employment and in media content we can support media and cultural organizations that address significant but neglected needs, sensibilities, and interests.

Promoting media literacy, media awareness, critical viewing and reading, and other media education efforts can constitute a fresh approach to the liberal arts and an essential educational objective on every level. CEM works to collect, publicize, and disseminate information, research, and evaluation about relevant programs, services, curricula, and teaching materials and helps to organize educational and parents' groups demanding pre-service and in-service teacher training in media analysis. This is already required in the schools of Australia, Canada, and Great Britain.

Finally, cultural policy issues must be placed on the social-political agenda. The CEM supports and, if necessary, organizes local and national media councils, study groups, citizen groups, minority and professional groups, and other forums of public discussion, policy development, representation, and action. It isn't a matter of waiting for a blueprint but of creating and experimenting with ways of community and citizen participation in local, national, and international media policy making. In this way we share experiences, lessons, and recommendations and, thus, gradually move towards a realistic democratic agenda.

The condition of the physical environment may determine how long our species survives. But it is the cultural environment that affects the quality of any survival. We need to begin the long process of diversifying, pacifying, democratizing, and humanizing the mainstream storytelling process that shapes the cultural environment in which we live and into which our children are born.

National Initiatives Can Help Address the Problem of Media Violence

by Sissela Bok

About the author: *Sissela Bok is a professor of population and development studies at Harvard University and the author of* Mayhem: Violence as Public Entertainment, *from which the following viewpoint is excerpted.*

As we consider the many approaches to deal with the influx of media violence in programs and games marketed for young people, the question arises: How might an entire society mobilize in response? Some societies offer few opportunities in this regard; in others, religious or political authorities impose policies from on high. It may be instructive to look at the experience of two democracies that have encouraged a broad-based public debate about how best to respond: Canada and Norway.

Canada's Campaign Against Media Violence

Canada offers an example of a nationwide effort to incorporate a focus on media literacy into a broad-gauged campaign to counter the effects of media violence. Canada has the second-highest homicide rates among industrialized democracies, after the United States; and U.S. media violence filters across Canada's borders without cease. The debate about how to deal with what many in the public regarded as excessive levels of screen violence had foundered repeatedly in the past on the issue of free speech versus censorship; and it had been impeded by a quest for the "definitive" study of the effects of media violence and the difficulty of bringing together the broadcasters, the cable industry, the educational and medical communities, regulators, producers, advertisers, and other interested parties to seek a solution all could accept.

Two events galvanized Canadians into action. In 1989, fourteen young women were shot to death at the École Polytechnique in Montreal. And a 13-year-old girl, Virginie Lariviere, whose sister had been raped and murdered, launched a national petition to ban all TV violence; by the time she presented it to the prime minister in 1992, more than 1.3 million signatures had been gathered.

The petition called for state regulation; but when the government took action, it chose instead to stress voluntary efforts on the part of media producers and consumers alike. It gave the Canadian Radio-television and Telecommunications Commission (CRTC) the mandate to engage every part of the society in considering the growing role of media violence in the lives of children and young people. Members of the commission engaged in wide-ranging discussions with private citizens old and young, with executives from the cable industry and from pay-TV and pay-per-view organizations, as well as representatives of Canada's Advertising Foundation, Teachers' Federation, Home and School and Parent-Teacher Federation, and other organizations. The commission also sponsored public colloquia and took part in meetings in the United States, Mexico, France, and other nations to explore common problems.

A Broad-Based Approach

In 1994, the Canadian broadcasting industry initiated pioneering field studies of the V-chip. The focus on this and other technological approaches to parental control represented only about 10 percent of the Canadian response to TV violence; by comparison, about 80 percent of the commission's effort was devoted to public education, including media literacy and the support of quality programming for children, and another 10 percent to establishing voluntary codes, agreed to by the Canadian entertainment industry, to ban excessive violence and to allow violence unsuited for children only after the "watershed hour" of nine P.M.

The Canadians recognized that the V-chip empowers parents to protect their children only if they choose to do so; more is needed to provide consumers with the knowledge and understanding to use their new power wisely. In the United States, by contrast, the V-chip is often debated in isolation from issues of media literacy, high-quality TV for children, and industry self-restraint, and it has therefore often been vested with extravagant symbolic meaning in the larger conflicts over entertainment violence. For some, it has conjured up hopes of near-magical powers for parents to regain control over what their children watch; others have dismissed it as tilting at windmills, or decried its deceptive appeal as a magic bullet that could permit par-

> *"When the [Canadian] government took action, it chose . . . to stress voluntary efforts on the part of media producers and consumers alike."*

ents and society to continue ignoring the real needs of their children.

Canada's approach presents a model for other societies to study as they seek to respond to public concern and to facilitate debate about measures to deal with media violence. It is a model, too, for building consensus and exploring alternative policies without being sidetracked by simplistic rationales and false dilemmas. It shows how cooperative discussions can serve an educational function for media representatives as well as for the general public, and it illustrates the advantages of making partial improvements over doing nothing. It demonstrates the possibility of cutting back on the amount of violence reaching children and of making possible broader changes, once the societal burden of media violence is recognized and shouldered by all who play a role in its production.

> *"About 80 percent of the [Canadian government's] effort was devoted to public education, including media literacy and the support of quality programming for children."*

Former CRTC chairman Keith Spicer describes this approach as "consensual and cooperative, not legalistic and coercive"—one that

> aims to keep program decision-making away from regulators and throw it back where it belongs, to thoughtful producers, script-writers, advertisers and distributors listening to more informed, better-equipped parents. . . . We believe that—as with pollution, drunk driving, and smoking—long-term public discussion can make obsessive violence directed at children socially unacceptable.

Norway's Approach to Combating Media Violence

The Norwegian government could draw on Canada's experience as it launched its own campaign, in 1993, "to combat violence in the visual media." This campaign was part of an even broader effort to deal with every aspect of societal violence. While under Nazi occupation during World War II, Norway had experienced the most stringent censorship and attempts to impose every other form of totalitarian control. A vibrant resistance movement had blunted these controls to some extent; but Norwegians had come to know firsthand, as few other democratic societies, the evils under regimes exercising such controls.

Five decades after the war, a new sort of resistance was needed. By the 1990s, violent crime was on the rise in Norway. Its rates were still among the world's lowest, but that was no reason for complacency. Young males in particular were turning to violence more often, and increasing numbers of elderly people, children, and women were beginning to fear for their safety. The campaign to resist violence in the visual media was only part of a larger public effort to bring about a "safer, warmer, and more just society with a higher quality of life" for all citizens. The aim, the organizers declared, was not only to reduce violence but to increase Norway's traditionally high levels of resilience, empathy, and community cohesiveness. Since viewers cannot change or react directly to the violent situations on the screen, the organizers warned, they may develop an emotionally passive remoteness to what they subsequently experience in real life:

> If our capacity to react to injustice and violence is weakened, we will get a colder society. Thus the way may be paved for an even greater increase of vio-

lence as an expression of frustration and the need for self-assertion, and as a means of conflict resolution in the local community and the family.

Among the aims of the campaign were to have the government work with citizen groups and the media to generate a "broad mobilization against violence in the media, to create awareness of the public's power and responsibility, to give priority to children and adolescents as a target group, [and] to place responsibility on those who disseminate media violence." The Norwegians also aimed to disseminate greater knowledge of the visual media and to foster greater understanding of the visual language, to enable consumers to make more critical and conscious use of the media. Such a campaign would require consistent efforts in the schools, as well as strengthened adult education courses in media literacy.

The planners of the campaign knew that Norway could not, by itself, guard against programming originating abroad. Therefore, they initiated broader contacts with other Scandinavian countries, with the European Council, and with organizations worldwide to facilitate greater international collaboration in dealing with media violence. But while recognizing the problems posed by the multiplying channels available to the public and seeking to meet these challenges, the authors of the Norwegian plan also rejected the view of those who find any technological innovation problematic. We must not forget, they insisted, the "fantastic possibilities for increased communication, knowledge, insight and new forms of interaction that the audiovisual media are opening up."

Guarding Against Overzealousness

It was equally important, the Norwegians believed, not to blame the media for every outbreak of violence. The temptation to do so was strong when, in the fall of 1994, a case arose that was reminiscent of the killing of James Bulger in Liverpool the year before. A five-year-old girl was found dead near her house in a suburb of Trondheim after having been beaten unconscious by three playmates, then abandoned in the snow. The public was incensed and quick to blame media violence. The commercial television channel TV3 canceled the series *Mighty Morphin Power Rangers*, which was already under heavy criticism for its violence. A search of the homes of the boys who had beaten the girl revealed, however, no violent videotapes; nor did they appear to have watched violent programs on TV. A few weeks later, the Mighty Morphins returned to the screen. Instead of censorship, community efforts were mobilized to help friends and neighbors deal with the shock. Inquiries were made into ways in which the girl's death could have been avoided; and a broad-ranging debate took place in the press about the different causative factors that interact in precipitating any act of violence and about ways for families, communities, and society to counter each one.

> *"[Canada's approach] illustrates the advantages of making partial improvements over doing nothing."*

In both Canada and Norway, the campaigns have taken longer than at first expected and are still far from having achieved fully adequate responses to the problems of media violence. But both societies are better prepared to deal with these problems than they would have been had they not undertaken to learn about them and to discuss different approaches to them with all interested parties.

> *"[Norway's] campaign to resist violence in the visual media was only part of a larger public effort to bring about a 'safer, warmer, and more just society.'"*

All who struggle to respond to the problem of media violence without leaping to overhasty conclusions—from the many groups active in the Canadian and Norwegian campaigns to the American second-graders who formulated their own "Declaration of Independence from Violence"—are concerned, at bottom, with achieving a measure of personal responsibility and independence that they see as endangered. [It is important to be aware of] the psychological and moral "failure to thrive" to which heavy exposure to media violence [can] contribute, through the effects of increased fear, desensitization, appetite for more violence, and aggression. For purposes of moving in the opposite direction, of protecting or enhancing a state of thriving, the choice must be to understand each of those effects in order to be able to reverse them; and to encourage, instead, greater resilience, empathy, self-control, and respect for self and others.

Actively Resisting Violence

When the Canadians and Norwegians speak of their campaigns as involving "antiviolence," I take them to have in mind not only guarding against the four effects but also moving to reverse each one. In these ways, their stance goes beyond that of nonviolence to one of active resistance to violence. Much as being active in the antislavery movement of the last century involved more than not engaging in slavery oneself, so joining in an antiviolence movement has to go beyond opting for nonviolence in one's personal life. It calls for engaging in imaginative and forceful practices of nonviolent *resistance* to violence, including taking a stand toward entertainment violence. There is a world of opportunities for anyone choosing to take such a stand. Cultures are not frozen in stone. Violence is taught, promoted, glamorized; it can be unlearned, resisted, deglamorized. In the continuing contest between initiatives that can either enhance or debilitate human prospects, the words of Mohandas Gandhi still hold promise:

> We are constantly astonished at the amazing discoveries in the field of violence. But I maintain that far more undreamed of and seemingly impossible discoveries will be made in the field of nonviolence.

Bibliography

Books

Martin Barker and Julian Petley, eds.	*Ill Effects: The Media-Violence Debate*. New York: Routledge, 1997.
Sissela Bok	*Mayhem: Violence as Public Entertainment*. Reading, MA: Addison-Wesley, 1998.
Laurent Bouzereau	*Ultraviolent Movies: From Sam Peckinpah to Quentin Tarantino*. Secaucus, NJ: Carol, 1996.
Joanne Cantor	*Mommy, I'm Scared: How TV and Movies Frighten Children and What We Can Do to Protect Them*. New York: Harcourt Brace, 1998.
Robert Coles	*The Moral Intelligence of Children*. New York: Random House, 1997.
Kathy Edgar	*Everything You Need to Know About Media Violence*. New York: Rosen, 1998.
Herbert N. Foerstel	*Banned in the Media: A Reference Guide to Censorship in the Press, Motion Pictures, Broadcasting, and the Internet*. Westport, CT: Greenwood, 1998.
Arnold P. Goldstein	*Violence in America: Lesson on Understanding the Aggression in Our Lives*. Palo Alto, CA: Davies-Black, 1996.
Jeffrey H. Goldstein, ed.	*Why We Watch: The Attractions of Violent Entertainment*. New York: Oxford University Press, 1998.
Dave Grossman and Gloria Degaetano	*Stop Teaching Our Kids to Kill: A Call to Action Against TV, Movie, and Video Game Violence*. New York: Random House, 1999.
James T. Hamilton, ed.	*Television Violence and Public Policy*. Ann Arbor: University of Michigan Press, 1998.
Stephen Hunter	*Violent Screen: A Critic's Thirteen Years on the Front Lines of Movie Mayhem*. Baltimore: Bancroft Press, 1995.
John Leonard	*Smoke and Mirrors: Violence, Television, and Other American Cultures*. New York: New Press, 1997.

Diane E. Levine — *Remote Control Childhood?: Combating the Hazards of Media Culture.* Washington, DC: National Association for the Education of Young Children, 1998.

Madeline Levine — *See No Evil: A Guide to Protecting Our Children from Media Violence.* San Francisco: Jossey-Bass, 1998.

Madeline Levine — *Viewing Violence: How Media Violence Affects Your Child's and Adolescent's Development.* New York: Doubleday, 1996.

Michael Medved — *Hollywood vs. America: Popular Culture and the War on Traditional Values.* New York: HarperCollins, 1992.

Michael Medved — *Saving Childhood: Protecting Our Children from the National Assault on Innocence.* New York: HarperCollins, 1998.

Phil Phillips and Joan Hake Robie — *Horror and Violence: The Deadly Duo in the Media.* Lancaster, PA.: Starburst, 1988.

W. James Potter — *On Media Violence.* Thousand Oaks, CA: Sage, 1999.

Ronin Ro — *Gangsta: Merchandizing the Rhymes of Violence.* New York: St. Martin's Press, 1996.

Kevin W. Saunders — *Violence as Obscenity: Limiting the Media's First Amendment Protection.* Durham, NC: Duke University Press, 1996.

Daniel M. Shea, ed. — *Mass Politics: The Politics of Popular Culture.* New York: St. Martin's, 1999.

Victoria Sherrow — *Violence and the Media: The Question of Cause and Effect.* Brookfield, CT: Millbrook Press, 1996.

Periodicals

Dan Andriacco — "V-Chips Short-Circuit Parental Responsibility," *U.S. Catholic*, June 1996.

CQ Researcher — "School Violence," October 9, 1998. Available from 1414 22nd St. NW, Washington, DC 20037.

Susan J. Douglas — "The Devil Made Me Do It: Is *Natural Born Killers* the Ford Pinto of Movies?" *The Nation*, April 5, 1999.

Anne P. Dupre — "Violence, Depravity, and the Movies: The Lure of Deviancy," *USA Today*, January 1999.

Laurie J. Flynn — "V-Chip and Ratings Are Close to Giving Parents New Power," *New York Times*, April 2, 1998.

Charles Gordon — "Much Ado About Violence," *Maclean's*, May 24, 1999.

Dave Grossman — "Trained to Kill," *Christianity Today*, August 10, 1998.

Gayle M.B. Hanson — "The Violent World of Video Games," *Insight on the News*, June 28, 1999. Available from 3600 New York Ave. NE, Washington, DC 20002.

Wendy Kaminer — "The Politics of Sanctimony," *American Prospect*, November 23, 1999.

Bibliography

Paul Keegan — "Culture Quake," *Mother Jones*, November/December 1999.

Joseph I. Leiberman and John McCain — "The No-Show Summit," *New York Times*, May 12, 1997.

John Leo — "Gunning for Hollywood," *U.S. News & World Report*, May 10, 1999.

David Link — "Fact About Fiction" *Reason*, March 1994.

Rob Long — "Hollywood, Littleton, and Us," *National Review*, July 26, 1999.

Mike Males — "Stop Blaming Kids and TV," *Progressive*, October 1997.

Mary Megee — "Media Literacy: The New Basic," *Education Digest*, September 1997.

Newsweek — "Moving Beyond the Blame Game," May 17, 1999.

Virgina Postrel — "Creative Matrix: What We Lose by Regulating Culture," *Reason*, August/September 1999.

Joshua Quittner — "Are Video Games Really So Bad?" *Time*, May 10, 1999.

Judith A. Reisman — "Cultivating Killers: Pop Culture Is Getting Away with Murder," *New American*, June 7, 1999. Available from 770 Westhill Blvd., Appleton, WI 54914.

Frank Rich — "Washington's Post-Littleton Looney Tunes," *New York Times*, June 19, 1999.

John Romano — "It's a Job for Parents, Not the Government," *Newsweek*, August 9, 1999.

Jane Rosenzweig — "Can TV Improve Us?" *American Prospect*, July/August 1999.

Peter Schweitzer — "Bad Imitation," *National Review*, December 31, 1998.

Katharine Q. Seelye — "Clinton Holds Youth Violence 'Summit,'" *New York Times*, May 11, 1999.

Scott Stossel — "The Man Who Counts the Killings," *Atlantic Monthly*, May 1997.

Ray Surette — "That's Entertainment?" *World & I*, September 1998.

David Thomson — "A Gore Phobia," *Esquire*, May 1997.

Daniel T. Wackerman — "God Forbid That Anything Remotely Lewd or Gratuitously Violent Should Appear on the Old Zenith," *America*, March 2, 1996.

Daniel B. Wood — "Gauging the Effects of Violent Video Games," *Christian Science Monitor*, May 7, 1999.

Tara Zahra — "Did Buffy Do It?" *The Nation*, July 19, 1999.

Organizations to Contact

The editors have compiled the following list of organizations concerned with the issues debated in this book. The descriptions are derived from materials provided by the organizations. All have publications or information available for interested readers. The list was compiled on the date of publication of the present volume; the information provided here may change. Be aware that many organizations take several weeks or longer to respond to inquiries, so allow as much time as possible.

American Academy of Child and Adolescent Psychiatry (AACAP)
3615 Wisconsin Ave. NW, Washington, DC 20016-3007
(202) 966-7300 • fax: (202) 966-2891
website: www.aacap.org

AACAP is the leading national professional medical association committed to treating the 7 to 12 million American youth suffering from mental, behavioral, and developmental disorders. It publishes the monthly *Journal of the American Academy of Child and Adolescent Psychiatry* and the reports "Children and TV Violence" and "Understanding Violent Behavior in Children and Adolescents."

American Civil Liberties Union (ACLU)
125 Broad St., 18th Floor, New York, NY 10004
(212) 549-2500 • fax: (212) 549-2646
website: www.aclu.org

The ACLU is a national organization that works to defend Americans' civil rights as guaranteed by the U.S. Constitution. It opposes the V-chip and the censoring of any form of speech, including media depictions of violence. The ACLU publishes and distributes the semiannual newsletter *Civil Liberties Alert*, policy statements, pamphlets, and reports which include "From Words to Weapons: The Violence Surrounding Our Schools" and "The ACLU on Violence Chip."

American Family Association (AFA)
PO Drawer 2440, Tupelo, MS 38803
(601) 844-5036 • fax: (601) 842-7798
website: www.afa.net

AFA opposes the proliferation of violence, profanity, vulgarity, and pornography in popular entertainment. It sponsors letter-writing campaigns to encourage television sponsors to support only quality programming, and it compiles statistics on how media violence affects society. The association's publications include books, videos, the monthly *AFA Journal*, and the *AFA Action Alert* newsletter.

Center for Media Literacy
4727 Wilshire Blvd., Suite 403, Los Angeles, CA 90010
(800) 226-9494
website: www.medialit.org

The Center for Media Literacy is a national advocacy organization that distributes educational materials and develops training programs for promoting critical thinking about the media in school classrooms, afterschool programs, parent education, religious and community centers, and in the home. It publishes numerous books, lesson plans, videos, and CD-ROMs about media literacy, including the video *Beyond Blame: Challenging Violence in the Media* and the book *Who's Calling the Shots: How to Respond Effectively to Children's Fascination with War Play and War Toys.*

Cultural Environment Movement
PO Box 31847, Philadelphia, PA 19104
(215) 204-6434
website: www.cemnet.org

Founded by media violence researcher George Gerbner, the Cultural Environment Movement is an international coalition of organizations and individuals united in working for gender equity and general diversity in mass media employment, ownership, and representation. It publishes a newsletter, the *Monitor,* and organizes research symposiums and advocacy meetings.

The Lion & Lamb Project
4300 Montgomery Ave., Suite 104, Bethesda, MD 20814
(301) 654-3091
website: www.lionlamb.org

Lion & Lamb is a national grassroots initiative that provides information to parents about the effects of violent entertainment, toys, and games on children's behavior. The organization works with parents, teachers, day care providers, and others to advocate a simple message: "Violence is not child's play." It publishes a newsletter and a parent action kit.

Media Awareness Network
1500 Merivale Rd., 3rd Floor, Nepean, ON K2E 6Z5 Canada
(800) 896-3342 • fax: (613) 224-1958
website: www.media-awareness.ca

The mission of the Media Awareness Network is to promote and support media education in Canadian schools, homes, and communities. Through its Internet site, it provides both curriculum-related media and Web literacy teaching materials for schools, and media awareness resources for community organizations. Available on the "Media Violence" section of its website are news updates, online articles, and a summary of the key events in the Canadian government's response to the problem.

Media Coalition
139 Fulton St., Suite 302, New York, NY 10038
(212) 587-4025 • fax: (212) 587-2436
website: www.mediacoalition.org

The Media Coalition defends the First Amendment right to produce and sell books, magazines, recordings, videotapes, and video games. It defends the American public's right to have access to the broadest possible range of opinion and entertainment, including works considered offensive or harmful due to their violent or sexually explicit nature. Media Coalition distributes to its members regular reports outlining the activities of Congress, state legislatures, and the courts on issues related to the First Amendment.

Media Education Foundation
26 Center St., Northampton, MA 01060
(800) 897-0089
website: www.mediaed.org

The Media Education Foundation is a nonprofit organization devoted to media research and production of resources to aid educators and others in fostering analytical media literacy. The foundation produces educational videos, including *The Killing Screens: Media and the Culture of Violence* and *Game over Gender, Race & Violence in Video Games.*

Mediascope
12711 Ventura Blvd., Suite 440, Studio City, CA 91604
(818) 508-2080 • fax: (808) 508-2088
website: www.mediascope.org

Mediascope is a national, nonprofit research and public policy organization working to raise awareness about the way media affect society. It encourages responsible depictions of social and health issues in film, television, the Internet, video games, advertising, and music. Among its many publications are *Video Games and Their Effects, National Television Violence Study,* and *More than a Movie: Ethics in Entertainment.*

National Coalition Against Censorship
275 Seventh Ave., New York, NY 10001
(212) 807-6222
website: www.ncac.org

NCAC is an alliance of nonprofit organizations working to educate the public about the dangers of censorship and how to oppose it. The coalition strives to create a climate of opinion hospitable to First Amendment freedoms. Its website contains articles, testimony, and new updates regarding censorship of violence in the media.

National Coalition on Television Violence (NCTV)
5132 Newport Ave., Bethesda, MD 20816
website: www.nctvv.org

NCTV is a research and education association dedicated to reducing the violence in films and television programming. It distributes information on the V-chip, ratings, reviews, and violence research, and also publishes the quarterly *NCTV News.*

National Institute on Media and the Family
606 24th Ave. S., Suite 606, Minneapolis, MN 55454
(888) 672-KIDS
website: www.mediaandthefamily.org

The institute is a national center for research, education, and information about the impact of the media on children and families. Its publications include the *1999 Video and Computer Game Report Card* and the fact sheet *Children and Media Violence.*

Parents Television Council (PTC)
PO Box 712067, Los Angeles, CA 90071-9934
(213) 621-2506
website: www.ParentsTV.org

PTC was established as a special project of the Media Research Center. Its goal is to bring America's demand for values-driven television programming to the entertainment industry. PTC produces an annual *Family Guide to Prime Time Television,* based on scientific monitoring and analysis generated from the Media Research Center's computerized Media Tracking System. The *Family Guide* profiles every sitcom and drama on the major television networks and provides information on subject matter that is inappropriate for children. PTC also publishes various reports, including *A Vanishing Haven: The Decline of the Family Hour.*

TV-Turnoff Network
1611 Connecticut Ave. NW, Suite 3A, Washington, DC 20009
(202) 887-0436 • fax: (202) 518-5560
e-mail: tvfa@essential.org • website: www.tvfa.org

The TV-Turnoff Network is a national nonprofit organization that encourages Americans to reduce the amount of television they watch in order to promote stronger families and communities. It sponsors the National TV-Turnoff Week, when more than 5 million people across the country go without television for seven days.

Websites

The Games Project
www.gamesproject.org

The Games Project, jointly sponsored by Mennonite Central Committee Ontario and Christian Peacemaker Teams, evaluates video games and provides its findings on its website in an effort to discourage violent game use and promote the use of nonviolent life-affirming games.

Index

150

Index

parental concerns on, 87–88
parental responsibility on, 26–28, 85,
  89–90
prevalence of, 18
profiting from foreign sales, 135
public concern over, 13–14
relationship with actual violence
  American public on, 63
    con, 41, 102–103, 108–109
  debate on, 14–15, 19
  vs. gun use, 47–48
  juvenile, 52–53
  liberal denials of, 32–33
  media industry admitting to, 115
  vs. personal responsibility, 104, 141
  studies supporting, 69–70, 54–55, 62
  youth on, 73–74
 as serious problem, 17
 see also movies; music; television
  violence; video games
Medved, Michael, 99
Mencken, H.L., 42
Merida, Kevin, 18
Mighty Joe Young (movie), 53
military
 using murder simulators, 67–68
Miller, Mark, 114
Minow, Newton, 116
"Mortal Kombat" (video game), 34
Motion Picture Association of America
 (MPAA), 111, 112
movies
 blame placed on, 72
 call for restraining violence in, 59–60
 copying killings from, 19, 34, 52–53, 56,
  122–23
 glamorizing guns, 57
 glamorizing violence, 33–34
 and media industry responsibility, 73
 people saying "no" to violent, 124–25
 portraying murder as sport, 52–53
 for preschoolers, 95, 96
 profitability from violent, 57–59
 violent themes in, 18–19
 see also media violence; ratings system
Moynihan, Daniel Patrick, 124
Murdoch, Rupert, 35
music
 affects attitudes and behavior, 63–64
 demonizing, 78
 destructive themes in, 64–65
 efforts to restrict harmful, 65–66
 Goth, 20–21
 marketing toward children, 94
 need for ratings system for, 100

parents' criticism of, 75–76
positive influences of, 76–78
and school shootings, 20, 61
violence against women in, 93–94
violent themes in, 14, 61–62
see also media violence

NAACP v. Claiborne Hardware, 38–39
Nantais, David E., 75
Nation (magazine), 47
National Association of Broadcasters
 (NAB) television code, 88, 89, 116
National Association of Theater Owners
 (NATO), 111
National Coalition Against Censorship
 (NCAC), 37
National Commission on the Causes and
 Prevention of Violence, 13
National Institute of Mental Health, 69
National Institute on Media and the Family,
 92, 93
National Research Council, 41, 102
Natural Born Killers (movie), 53
 imitated in real life, 56
 lawsuits against, 114, 120, 121
 rating of, 58
news media
 crime overrepresented in, 133
 cultivating "mean world syndrome," 30
 distorting reality, 30–31
 influence on children, 96, 97
 violence in, 123
Nielsen rating, 26, 134
Nielson, Josh, 74
Nine Inch Nails, 93, 94
Norway, 140–42

O'Donnell, Rosie, 56
Osbourne, Ozzy, 76
Owens, Bill, 61

parental bill of rights, 72
parents
 breaking circle of blame, 126
 concerns about media influence on
  children, 87–88
 criticism of music, 75–76
 determining child's violent behavior, 54
 government efforts cannot replace, 110
 protecting children from media violence,
  26–28, 97–98
 raising boys, 80
 restricting children's access to media
  violence, 85
 supervisory responsibility of, 89–90

153